THE
Charter School
Challenge

THE
Charter School
Challenge

Avoiding the Pitfalls, Fulfilling the Promise

BRYAN C. HASSEL

BROOKINGS INSTITUTION PRESS
Washington, D.C.

ABOUT BROOKINGS

The Brookings Institution is a private nonprofit organization devoted to research, education, and publication on important issues of domestic and foreign policy. Its principal purpose is to bring knowledge to bear on current and emerging policy problems. The Institution maintains a position of neutrality on issues of public policy. Interpretations or conclusions in Brookings publications should be understood to be solely those of the authors.

Copyright © 1999
THE BROOKINGS INSTITUTION
1775 Massachusetts Avenue, N.W., Washington, D.C. 20036
www.brookings.edu

Library of Congress Cataloging-in-Publication data

Hassel, Bryan C.
    The charter school challenge : avoiding the pitfalls,
fulfilling the promise / Bryan C. Hassel.
        p.   cm.
    Includes bibliographical references and index.

    ISBN 0-8157-3512-X (cloth : perm. paper)
    ISBN 0-8157-3511-1 (pbk. : perm. paper)
    1. Charter schools—United States. 2. Charter schools—Political
aspects—United States. I. Title.
    LB2806.36 .H37   1999   98-58132
    371.01—dc21   CIP

                    9 8 7 6 5 4 3 2 1

The paper used in this publication meets minimum requirements of the American National Standard for Information Sciences—Permanence of Paper for Printed Library Materials: ANSI Z39.48-1984.

Typeset in Minion

Composition by Cynthia Stock
Silver Spring, Maryland

Printed by R. R. Donnelley and Sons
Harrisonburg, Virginia

Acknowledgments

MANY INDIVIDUALS and institutions contributed to this project with ideas, resources, or encouragement—some provided all three. Paul Peterson, Tom Loveless, and Alan Altshuler helped shape the work from the beginning, generating advice and insights without which this book would never have been completed. Others, including James Cibulka, Nancy Davidson, Robert Maranto, and Eric Rofes, provided thoughtful commentary on part or all of the manuscript. Research assistance from Margaret Certain, Ashley Houseman, and Joanne Scharer was invaluable. At the Brookings Institution Press, Janet Mowery provided editorial support, Carlotta Ribar proofread the pages, and Sherry Smith composed the index.

Because the study relied so heavily on empirical field research, I owe special thanks to the many people involved with charter school programs in Colorado, Georgia, Massachusetts, and Michigan who generously took time out of their busy schedules to answer my questions, search out documents, or otherwise provide information. I would particularly like to acknowledge the willingness of charter school founders and staff to make time for me—these folks have much more important matters on their minds than the inquiries of researchers.

The Kennedy School's Taubman Center for State and Local Government provided the initial financial support that made the project possible. Along with the Program on Education Policy and Governance, a joint venture between the Taubman Center and Harvard's Department of Government, the center extended the funding needed to conduct the research. The study also received generous financial support from the Aspen Institute's Nonprofit Sector Research Fund.

Three generations of family also deserve special mention. My parents, themselves both teachers by profession, taught me directly and by example to love learning and to finish a difficult job. My wife, Emily, talked me out of self-doubt a thousand times, even as she half-jokingly expressed an impatience that every writer needs to hear in order to finish. Though my children, Margaret and Christopher, provided more distractions than contributions, how could I not acknowledge their wonderful arrivals, each at critical times in the project's timeline?

To all of these people and the many others to whom I am grateful, I extend much-deserved thanks.

Contents

TABLES

FIGURES

THE
Charter School
Challenge

1 Charter Schools: The Promise and the Pitfalls

THE EMERGENCE and spread of charter schools in the United States was one of the most significant developments in public education in the 1990s. When 1991 began, no state had passed charter school legislation. By the end of 1998, 34 states and the District of Columbia had charter school legislation on the books. More than 1,100 charter schools were educating over 250,000 students.[1] By allowing citizens to start new public schools (or convert existing ones), freeing the schools from state laws and school district policies, and holding them accountable for results and "customer" satisfaction, proponents hope charter school programs will stimulate the formation of promising new educational options for children. And if the state money that would have paid for children to attend conventional schools follows them to charter schools, advocates argue that the programs will place competitive pressure on regular public schools and spur systemwide improvement.

Media reports often seem awestruck by the rapid spread of charter schools. The *Washington Post:* "Few ideas in American education today are building as much momentum as charter schools." *Time* magazine, in a cover story: "The charter movement is being heralded as the latest and

1

best hope for a public-education system that has failed to deliver for too many children and cannot compete internationally." *Education Week:* "In the past four years, the charter school concept has had the makings of a legislative juggernaut. . . . Democrats and Republicans alike are hot for the idea, and thousands of applicants have put in their bids to open schools under the new laws." *Phi Delta Kappan:* "Over the past few years charter schools have sometimes seemed to take on the aura of a 'silver bullet'—a magical solution to a variety of problems. The concept has been accepted by governors and legislators from both parties."[2]

Charter schools have become such a national phenomenon because they appear to sidestep two of the long standing barriers to improvement in American public education. The first of these is politics. U.S. public schools are battlegrounds on which political interests and factions fight for advantage. In that context, agreement on the ends and means of public education is elusive. Reforms that seem to have promise often fall victim to the crossfire of political debate. The second barrier is the practical difficulty of making reform work in public school systems. There are thousands of public school districts, all of them relatively independent from state and national government. Edicts from state capitals or Washington may have little or no effect on these semi-autonomous units. Even within school districts, system leaders often find it difficult to make reform happen in classrooms, which are themselves only loosely controlled by the central office. And even when an idea for improvement wins political victory in a state legislature or in Congress, the prospects for its successful implementation are bleak.

Charter schools seem like a reform that can get around both of those obstacles. In politics, charter schools have pressed both Republican and Democratic buttons. Republicans find them appealing because they provide public schools with a limited amount of competition, operate without some of the onerous burdens of regulation, and must produce acceptable educational results as a condition for continued funding. Some also believe charter schools can serve as a stepping-stone to more full-blown systems of school choice that include religious and other private schools. For their part, Democrats like the fact that charter schools create new options while adhering to the core values of public schooling (they are nonselective in their admissions, tuition-free, and nonreligious).

And some regard charter schools as a compromise that will help stave off calls for wider school choice. With their appeal on both sides of the aisle, charter schools have managed to muster bipartisan majorities in many states. Once in place, charter schools also operate with some insulation from the political turmoil that often surrounds public schools. Though ultimately accountable to some public authority, charter schools in theory are governed by independent boards with a great deal of autonomy. Because their curriculums, teaching methods, and management practices affect only those who choose to attend, charter schools do not have to convince districtwide majorities that their approaches are right. Arguably, moving decisions from the district to the school can diffuse the conflict that seems endemic to public education.

Charter schools also appear to sidestep the difficulties of implementing reform in the highly decentralized American education system. Rather than mandating change in existing schools, policymakers simply invite education entrepreneurs to come forward with new ideas, create a process for selecting the most promising proposals, and institute a system for holding the selected schools accountable for results. No unwilling superintendents or school boards have to be convinced; no recalcitrant faculties have to be retrained or redirected in their efforts; no parent organizations have to be told that their schools are changing in ways they do not like. If traditional public schools make changes in response to charter programs, they do so not at the behest of policymakers but in order to compete.

But will these programs live up to their promise? The same press reports with the hyperbolic tributes to charter schools' momentum are also filled with warnings and worries. The same *Education Week* piece that marveled at charter schools' "legislative juggernaut" fretted a few paragraphs later: "The history of education reform is littered with ideas that shine brightly and reap hosannas from all, only to flame out into a black hole of obscurity. Could charter schools follow the same trajectory?"[3]

In some ways, it is too early to say whether this fate has befallen charter programs. The oldest of the nation's charter schools opened in 1992; most have operated for two years or less. Improvements in the achievement of students who attend charter schools will probably take longer than that to show up. And "second-order effects"—changes in school districts in response to the presence or possibility of charters—will likely take even longer to manifest themselves.

But with charter laws on the books in more than 30 states and three or more years of implementation in more than 15 states, it is possible to begin investigating whether charter schools have avoided the pitfalls that have tripped up so many other education reforms. The first part of this study examines the politics of charter schools in state legislatures. Though more than half the states have passed charter school laws, how true have these statutes been to the charter school idea? What compromises have proponents had to strike in order to win passage? And why have some states compromised more than others? The second part of the study traces the effect of the legislative compromises on the implementation of charter school programs. Have the deals that made adoption possible also made effective implementation impossible? What other problems have bedeviled the rollout of charter school programs? The final part looks to the future, examining changes in the policy and practice of charter schools that would help improve their chances of success.

Charter Schools: Origins, Ideas, and Research

Tracing the intellectual roots of the charter school idea is difficult. Many observers credit Ray Budde with coining the term "charter" in the educational context. In his book *Education by Charter: Restructuring School Districts*, he proposes to empower teams of teachers to develop "educational charters": comprehensive plans for educational ventures that they would present to local school boards for endorsement.[4] Once approved, the teams would gain control of a budget and play a role in selecting teachers and staff. Others point to the Philadelphia school district, which in 1988 began experimenting with significant school restructuring known as "chartering."[5] Still others point abroad to Great Britain's 1988 Education Reform Act, which gave local schools the opportunity to "opt out" of local school jurisdictions and become part of a sort of national school district.[6]

Those early ideas contained some important elements of what we now call charter schools—teams of people starting from scratch in the design of new schools; site-level control over key decisions; evaluation of the venture's results—but the full-blown charter concept grew out of numerous movements for education reform. Five were especially important: (1) the push for more *choice* for students: giving every child a voucher or tax credit that he or she could use to attend any school, public or private; (2) the related idea of *competition*: breaking school districts' monopoly over the provision of education; (3) *school-based management*: delegating key school decisions to schools and classrooms; (4) the related push for *deregulation*: eliminating many of the rules constraining practice in schools; and (5) calls for greater *accountability for results*: setting high academic standards for schools and students and establishing consequences tied to performance.[7]

Many observers would argue that it was Ted Kolderie who brought all of these ideas together to create the charter school concept. Kolderie's "nine essentials" form the core of the charter idea:[8]

1. The school may be organized, owned, and run by any of several parties.

2. The organizers may approach more than one public body for their charter.

3. The school is a legal entity.

4. The school is public (that is, it is nonreligious, does not charge tuition, cannot discriminate or engage in selective admissions, and must follow health and safety laws).

5. The school accepts accountability for the students' academic performance; the school loses its charter if it fails to achieve its goals.

6. The school gets real freedom to change instructional and management practices.

7. The school is a school of choice: no student is required to attend.

8. The state transfers a fair share of school funding from each student's home district to the charter school.

9. Teachers are protected (that is, given leaves of absence to teach in charter schools and remain in the retirement system) and given new opportunities to participate in the design of schools.[9]

How might such arrangements lead to the improvement of education?[10] To understand the argument, it helps to think of charter programs as operating on two levels. On one level, the programs create a new institutional regime for the charter schools themselves. Whereas conventional schools are bound by pages of regulations stipulating what and how they teach, where they spend their money, whom they may hire and fire, and so on, charter schools are granted substantial autonomy. Principally, this is autonomy regarding the *means* they employ to attain their educational objectives. They can choose their own curriculum and materials, hire teachers without conventional certification, spend their budgets as they see fit, and the like. They also have some autonomy regarding the *ends* they pursue, though their formal goals must be approved by public authorities. This autonomy frees the schools to exhibit the responsiveness charter advocates regard as essential, allows educators to exercise their professional judgment, and limits red tape.

Charter schools are not just freer to be responsive and to work hard, however. They also have incentives to do so. One incentive comes from the fact that charter schools are "schools of choice." No student is compelled to attend a charter school; parents may withdraw their children from charter schools at any time. Charter schools cannot take their "customers" for granted. Their very survival depends upon the degree to which families believe the schools are responding to family preferences and working hard to provide the education they demand. Another incentive comes from charter schools' contractual obligation to the public, which is embodied in their charters. No charter is permanent. Whatever public authority oversees charter schools can close down any institution that fails to achieve the standards it agreed to in its charter. It stands to reason, the argument goes, that the average charter school will be more responsive and exert more effort than the average conventional school. Further, those that do not will go out of business, either because they fail to attract enough students or because the regulatory authority revokes their charters.

Charter school programs also change the institutional structure on a broader level by affecting the incentives of existing school districts. As charter proponent Ted Kolderie writes: "The intent is not simply to produce a few new and hopefully better schools. It is to create dynamics that will cause the main-line system to change so as to improve education for all students."[11] The primary dynamic is competitive pressure on conventional schools. Charter school advocates say that school districts without charter school programs find it easier to ignore demands for responsiveness and change than to fulfill them because saying no has few negative consequences. Where charter school programs are in place, those who seek changes (principals, teachers, families, community members) have a potential alternative: they can start (or join) a charter school. If others share their preferences, this alternative can impose real costs on school districts, because public funding follows students who opt for charter schools. Thus districts will be more likely to say yes to ideas for change and to generate their own ideas.

Another potential dynamic is that charter schools will serve as laboratories for new educational ideas. Without the constraints imposed by state laws and school district policies, they may try out new approaches. Those that succeed can be exported to existing schools for broader adoption. The laboratory might function on a system level as well, as the techniques public bodies develop to oversee charter schools and hold them accountable for results produce lessons for the regulation of public schools more generally. The laboratory function is highlighted in the statements of legislative intent of several state charter school laws and by some authors, but charter advocates like Kolderie do not emphasize it.[12] The laboratory idea emerges from a different diagnosis of the problem with American schooling, a diagnosis that focuses on the difficulties of generating "good ideas" in the current system. Kolderie argues, by contrast, that the system is bedeviled not by a lack of good ideas per se but by a lack of incentives to capitalize upon them.

A final possibility is that charter schools will transform public education not by inducing regular schools to change or by generating good ideas but simply by replacing conventional public schools as the primary providers of public education. This scenario draws on arguments such as those of John E. Chubb and Terry M. Moe, who have suggested that political forces make it difficult or impossible for conventional school districts to create high-performing schools.[13] Accordingly, regular schools will not be able to change sufficiently to stop the outflow of students. Families will exit the system until most students receive their education through charter schools.

Of course, not everyone accepts the argument that charter schools have transformative powers. Detractors argue that charter schools will

Figure 1-1. *Number of States with Charter School Laws at Year End, 1991–97*

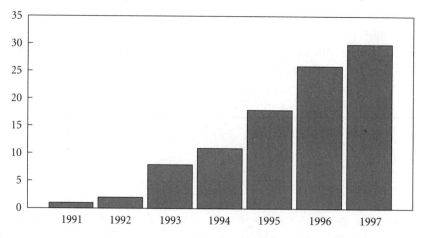

Source: RPP International, *A National Study of Charter Schools: Second-Year Report* (Washington; U.S. Office of Educational Research and Improvement, 1998), p. 10.

cream off the best and most motivated students, leaving regular public schools unable to compete; that they will become bastions of race and class segregation; that, exempted from rules, they will engage in actions that other schools' rules are designed to prevent, like discrimination, mistreatment of handicapped children, financial misconduct, or simply shoddy educational practice; that they will siphon off energy and re-sources that could be devoted to improving other public schools; or that they will serve too few students to make a difference.

These criticisms notwithstanding, state legislatures from all regions of the country have adopted charter laws. Minnesota passed the first charter school law in 1991. California followed in 1992. The next year saw six new laws, and the number of states with charter statutes has grown dramatically since then (see Figures 1-1 and 1-2). As Chapter 2 describes, these laws differ greatly from one another. None lives up entirely to Kolderie's nine essentials. But the broad idea of charter schools has caught on and spread rapidly. In the wake of state laws, charter schools have sprung up across the country. Figure 1-3 charts the growth in the number of charter schools since the first one opened its doors in 1992. Table 1-1

Figure 1-2. *States with Charter School Laws, December 1998*[a]

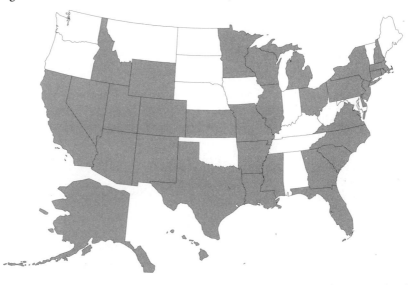

Source: Center for Education Reform, "Charter School Highlights and Statistics," published on the center's website: http://edreform.com.

a. Shaded states have charter school laws. Although not visible on this map, the District of Columbia also has a charter school law.

displays the number of charter schools in operation in each state at the start of the 1998–99 school year.

Not surprisingly, the growth of the charter movement has spawned a great deal of discussion in the press and in think tanks.[14] Much of this work has focused on explaining the charter concept, characterizing the first charter laws, and relating stories of early implementation. In addition, quite a few publications make the case for charter school programs, notably Kolderie's *Beyond Choice to New Public Schools* and Kolderie, Robert Lerman, and Charles Moskos's "Educating America."[15] The most comprehensive is Joe Nathan's *Charter Schools*, which includes historical material, arguments for charter school laws, and practical advice for charter organizers.[16]

Because the movement is in its infancy, the most sophisticated analyses have primarily examined charter school statutes rather than imple-

Figure 1-3. *Approximate Number of Charter Schools in Operation, 1992–93 to 1998–99*

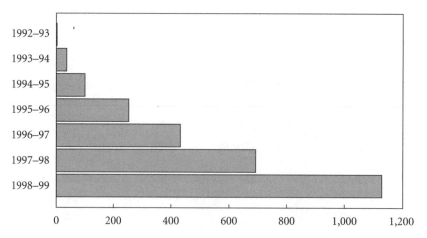

Sources: Data from 1992–93 through 1997–98 from RPP International, *A National Study of Charter Schools*, p. 10. With the exception of the 1997–98 data, these data represent the cumulative number of charter schools that had opened by the end of the school year in question. They do not take account of school closings. As of September 1997, the study reports, 19 schools . had closed. The 1997–98 and 1998–99 data represent the number of schools in operation at the beginning of the school year in question. The 1998–99 figure is from the Center for Education Reform, "Charter School Highlights and Statistics."

mentation.[17] But as experience has developed, studies have included information about critical implementation challenges. An early effort by the U.S. General Accounting Office highlighted the potential mismatch between charter school autonomy and federal categorical funding programs.[18] Chester E. Finn, Bruno V. Manno, and Louann Bierlein's report on the seven states with the most charter activity brought to the fore many of the startup issues faced by charter school initiatives and provides the most comprehensive accounting to date of what is happening in the largest state programs. The same group's follow-up study extended the analysis to even more states.[19] Other useful research has studied and evaluated programs in early-adopting states.[20] The U.S. Department of Education launched a major research effort in charter schools in 1995, which is referred to in this book as "the national charter school

Table 1-1. *Charter Schools in Operation, by State, 1998–99 School Year*

State	Number	State	Number
Alaska	17	Michigan	139
Arizona	271	Minnesota	35
California	156	Mississippi	1
Colorado	61	Nevada	1
Connecticut	16	New Jersey	31
Delaware	4	New Mexico	5
District of Columbia	19	North Carolina	59
Florida	75	Ohio	15
Georgia	27	Pennsylvania	31
Hawaii	2	Rhode Island	2
Illinois	14	South Carolina	5
Kansas	15	Texas	60
Louisiana	10	Wisconsin	24
Massachusetts	34	Total	1,129

Source: Center for Education Reform, "Charter School Highlights and Statistics," September 1998, published on the center's website: http://edreform.com.

study."[21] And reports have begun to emerge on specific aspects of the charter experience, such as their impact on local schools and school districts and student achievement and accountability in charter schools.[22]

Together, these studies have produced some interesting findings in three primary areas. First, they have provided a statistical profile of charter schools and the students who attend them. For example, we now know that:

—Most charter schools are small. The median enrollment in 1996–97 was 150; it was 500 in other public schools in states with charter schools. More than 60 percent enrolled fewer than 200 students; only 16 percent of regular public schools had fewer than 200 students.

—Three in five charter schools are brand new institutions. A quarter are conversions of existing public schools. And 13 percent are conversions of existing private schools.

—On average, charter schools serve student populations that are fairly similar to those in their states. In charter schools, about 42 percent of students were nonwhite in 1996–97, about 40 percent in the existing public schools of 16 charter states. Some 36 percent of charter students were eligible for a free or reduced-priced lunch (a common indicator of poverty), about 40 percent in the regular public schools.[23]

These aggregate numbers mask some differences from state to state and from school to school. For example, the national study reports that a third of charter schools serve a distinctively higher percentage of non-white students than their surrounding districts. And in some states, like Texas, very high percentages of charter schools serve largely nonwhite populations.[24]

Second, charter school legislation varies from one state to the next. Some charter laws closely approximate the ideal charter legislation envisioned by charter school advocates; others contain so many compromises that they bear little resemblance to the vision laid out by Kolderie and other charter-idea pioneers. Many analyses categorize state laws as "strong" or "weak" and "live" or "dead," depending upon their faithfulness to the charter idea.[25] Others rank charter school laws on a scale of "strength" or "permissiveness."[26] These differences and their political origins are the subject of Chapters 2 and 3.

Third, research has illuminated some of the central difficulties charter schools have faced in this early phase of development. According to the national charter school study, seven out of ten charter schools had difficulty acquiring the resources they needed to start up or operate. Among the most common problems were lack of startup funds, lack of planning time, inadequate operating funds, and inadequate facilities. Aside from resource limitations, the second most common cluster of problems was resistance or opposition from outside organizations: state and local boards of education, state departments of education, local school districts, and educators' unions.[27] These problems, it should be said, were cited by schools that actually managed to open their doors. In many states with charter school laws on the books, only a small number of charter schools have managed to gain approval to open. In those states, the primary problems facing charter school programs have not been the operational ones cited in the U.S. Education Department's study, but the unwillingness of public bodies like school districts to issue charters.

Plan of the Book

This chapter began with the contention that charter schools may hold special promise as an education reform, exhibiting an ability to win rare bipartisan political support and to bypass some of the conventional implementation challenges that have tripped up previous reforms. This brief summary of the research on charter schools, though, dwells more on pitfalls than on promise. Though charter schools have achieved impressive bipartisan backing, the significant compromises made in many states have resulted in a host of charter laws that look much different from the charter school idea. And though charter schools sidestep some implementation difficulties, they have encountered others. Furthermore, the political and implementation issues faced by charter school programs may well be related. To what extent are political compromises struck by state legislatures responsible for the implementation difficulties encountered by charter school programs?

The rest of this book delves into these issues in more detail. By examining the politics of charter schools, I hope to provide an understanding of the political dynamics that have produced the wide variation in charter laws from one state to the next. I begin by providing a "bird's-eye view" of the basic political characteristics that have predicted the adoption of charter laws in the 50 states, as well as the adoption of "stronger" charter laws. This analysis reveals some interesting patterns, but it ultimately raises more questions than it answers. In particular, it gives us little feel for the processes through which charter school legislation has been made, the processes that have produced the vast differences we see from state to state. So the next chapter analyzes in more depth the details of charter school policymaking in four states with early charter laws: Colorado, Georgia, Massachusetts, and Michigan. These case studies provide a closer look at charter school politics and a better understanding of why these processes have had different results in different states.

The second part of the book turns to the implementation of charter laws in the same four states. Though it is too early to tell whether these fledgling programs have been "successful" in the full sense of the word, it is possible to discern whether some basic conditions are in place for success. I examine in turn whether the programs are granting charter schools the sort of autonomy that charter proponents ask for, whether the programs are designed so that charter schools have the resources to be viable as institutions, and whether the programs have the *potential*, at least, to have an impact on the broader system of public education through the competition they exert and the models they create. The three chapters in this part address to what extent the political compromises struck in the legislative process have adversely affected the ability of the programs to live up to these conditions.

The picture painted by these chapters is not a bright one. Political compromises and their accompanying implementation problems have severely hampered the ability of charter school programs to live up to their promise as an educational reform. But the final chapter looks to the future. Drawing on the early experience of charter school programs, I explore how charter schools might capitalize on their promise after all.

The Politics of Charter School Programs

I

2 | A Bird's-Eye View of Charter School Politics

DESPITE SOME common threads, charter school laws across the country differ from one another so greatly that they appear to have been cut from different fabrics altogether. One set of laws, termed "strong laws" or "live laws" by charter school proponents, empowers a wide variety of groups to start charter schools; allows these groups to petition some entity other than the local school board to obtain charter status; gives charter schools wide latitude in their curriculums, teaching practices, and operations; and authorizes the creation of a large number of the new institutions. Another set, known as "weak" or "dead" laws, restricts the range of groups eligible to propose charter schools, often to existing public schools; grants local school boards veto power over charter schools in their jurisdictions; allows only minimal independence and latitude; or strictly limits the number of charter schools that may open.[2]

In addition to these variations, of course, 16 states had not enacted any sort of charter legislation, weak or strong, by the end of 1998. The bird's-eye view of charter school politics provided in this chapter looks at what political variables distinguish charter states from noncharter states and weak states from strong ones. This analysis uncovers a few interesting patterns and challenges at least one piece of conventional wisdom about charter school politics.

Variations in Charter School Laws

As of January 1996, eleven states had charter school laws on the books (see Table 2-1). Though states have continued to adopt laws (and will probably do so for the next few years), this analysis focuses on the relatively early adopters of charter school laws. As more and more states adopt charter laws, fewer characteristics will differentiate charter states from noncharter states.

To differentiate strong from weak statutes, this analysis focuses on five characteristics of charter school laws that seem most important to the ultimate success of charter school programs and that set state laws apart from one another.[3]

First, did the charter law empower some public body other than local school boards to authorize charter schools? The strongest laws enabled several different entities to approve charter schools, helping to lower barriers to entry. The weakest laws allowed only the local school board to approve charters, a restriction that likely limits the potential for innovation and significant competition. Second, did the law allow a wide range of individuals and groups to propose charter schools? The strongest laws invited almost any citizen or organization, with the exception of religious organizations, to make proposals. The weakest laws allowed only existing public schools to apply for conversion to charter status.

Third, did the charter law grant charter schools significant legal and fiscal independence from local school districts? The strongest laws established charter schools as legally separate entities and provided funds directly to charter schools. The weakest laws made charter schools legally and fiscally part of existing school districts. Fourth, did the charter law exempt charter schools automatically from a wide range of public school laws and regulations? The strongest laws did so; the weakest allowed exemptions in only a few cases or required charter schools to ask for exemptions on a case-by-case basis. Finally, did the law make it possible for a large number of charter schools to open? The strongest laws placed no limits (or high limits) on the number of schools and provided charter schools with enough resources to make them financially viable. The weakest strictly limited the number of charter schools or provided the schools with inadequate resources.

These five characteristics appear most important to the success of the charter school idea and distinguished state charter school laws from one another. Without this second criterion, a sixth feature would surely be added to this list: the extent to which charter school laws held charter schools accountable for producing acceptable academic results. No charter school law could be regarded as strong unless it included provisions to ensure that only successful charter schools survive, provisions that are as essential to the charter idea as those regarding autonomy. But state charter school laws as enacted showed very little variation on this issue. Some required the students in charter schools to take state tests; others did not. Charter laws specified somewhat different procedures for revoking and renewing charters. But on the core issues of accountability—limiting the terms of charters, stating the grounds upon which charters can be revoked, and laying out the essential criteria for removal—charter laws looked very similar.

The exceptions were the laws in Arizona and Michigan that allowed charter terms of 10 to 15 years; in most other charter states the term was three to six years.[4] This distinction, however, does not warrant the inclusion of accountability provisions in an analysis of how the first 20 state laws differ, for two reasons. First, though two of these laws allowed longer charters, they each required a review every five to seven years. As a practical matter, low-performing charter schools in all states were at equal risk of having their charters revoked. Second, those two jurisdictions would be regarded as having strong laws even if they were weak on this one dimension. The analysis that follows would not turn out any differently if accountability provisions were included in the list of features worth considering.

Table 2-1 shows how each state law addressed the five issues. Although each law can fall somewhere on a continuum from strong to weak, the table classifies each state as either strong or weak on each dimension.

One state—Arizona—possessed all five attributes of strong laws. Six others possessed four of the five. These seven were unquestionably at

Table 2-1. *Provisions of 20 State Charter School Laws*[a]

	Classification																			
	Strong																*Weak*			
Provision	AZ	MI	DE	NJ	TX	CA	NH	MA	MN	CO	AK	HI	LA	WY	AR	GA	KS	NM	RI	WI
Entity other than local board may authorize a charter school	•	•	•	•	•	•	•	•	•	•								•	•	
Wide range of people and organizations may start a charter school	•		•		•	•	•	•	•	•	•	•	•	•				•		•
Charter school may be legally and fiscally independent of local school board	•	•	•	•	•	•	•	•				•								
Charter school receives automatic exemption from broad range of state and local policies	•	•	•		•	•	•	•	•	•	•	•	•							
Law enables many charter schools to open	•	•	•	•	•	•				•	•	•	•	•	•	•				

Sources: States with charter laws from RPP International, *A National Study of Charter Schools: Second-Year Report* (Washington: U.S. Department of Education, 1998).

a. The 20 states in this table had passed charter laws by the end of January 1996. Coding of state laws on various dimensions is based on the author's analysis of state statutes as they initially passed their state legislatures. Many of these laws have subsequently been amended. Details are available from the author on request.

the "strong" end of the continuum. Three states—Massachusetts, Minnesota, and Colorado—possessed three strong characteristics each. This analysis considers them strong, however, because they had what many observers regard as the most essential characteristic of strong laws: the availability of an authorizer other than the local school board.[5] On the weak side of the line were ten states with two or fewer strong characteristics. Two of these states—New Mexico and Rhode Island—empowered some entity other than the local school board to authorize charter schools. But the absence of any other strong provisions renders these laws weak.

Political Factors

What political factors lead some states to adopt weaker charter school laws than others? Presumably, the extent of compromise depends upon the legislative balance between proponents and opponents of the proposed reform. The stronger the opponents, the more compromised a reform is likely to be after churning through the legislative process. Among the potential indicators of power in state policymaking in general and education policymaking in particular are partisan balance, the power of teachers' organizations, objective educational conditions, and political culture.

Partisan Balance

States have increasingly become partisan battlegrounds.[6] Although parties have long battled for control of state policymaking, the number of states in which one party was more or less assured of control has declined since the 1970s.[7]

One aspect of partisan control is the balance of power in state legislatures, which are often regarded as the central players in education policymaking.[8] But the literature on state policymaking in general, and on education policymaking in particular, also points to the importance of the governor. As they have gained the power to stay in office longer, to initiate budgets, to veto legislation, and to hire larger staffs, governors have become much more effective in policymaking, especially as policy

Ralph Perpich *discussion group.*

innovators.[9] Perhaps nowhere has their heightened profile been more evident than in the education arena, where since the 1980s governors have played a larger role in framing and resolving policy debates.[10]

In popular discussions of the politics of charter schools, the reform is widely regarded as "bipartisan," appealing to both Republicans and Democrats.[11] Republicans may see charter schools as an imperfect but still promising step on the road to their desired system of school governance, in which public dollars follow students to the schools they choose, public or private. By contrast, Democrats may regard charter schools as a way to encourage experimentation and limit family choice, perhaps staving off calls for more radical "market" reforms in the process. If this bipartisan story is right, one would not expect differences in the balance of party power to distinguish charter from noncharter states. But although both Democrats and Republicans may support charter legislation of some kind, Republicans are more likely to favor strong charter laws. Strong charter laws more closely resemble the broader school choice that Republicans tend to favor.[12]

Power of Teachers' Organizations

Beyond the partisan balance in state legislatures and governors' mansions, one might also examine the power of relevant interest groups in state politics, which have become more and more important state-level actors.[13] Of course, interest groups exert power in part through their influence on the partisan balance, so this variable is not wholly separable from the previous one. But interest groups also wield power through lobbying and other political campaigns.

Historically, state-level battles over education pitted "schoolmen," proponents of expanding funding for universal public education, against elements opposed to such expansion. It was these broad-based coalitions interested in expanding the "pie," rather than more narrowly focused interest groups intent on getting bigger "slices," that defined state-level education politics.[14] Increasingly, though, observers have noted the progressive fragmentation of interest groups, though they still mobilize for collective action in times of crisis.[15] A great deal of this attention has focused on educators' unions, which have much more influence in state politics than they used to. Contrast the remark of Bailey and others, who argued in the early 1960s that unions had little influence at the state level except as witnesses in legislative hearings, with Thomas and Hrebenar's 1996 analysis of state-level interest-group activity. This survey of political knowledgeables found that the schoolteachers' union was ranked "most effective" in 43 of the 50 states. Only business groups ranked "most effective" in anywhere near as many states (36). No other group earned this rating in more than 26 states.[16]

In many places, teachers' unions have led the fight against charter school laws; in others, they have pressed for the passage of weak state laws.[17] Charter schools run against union positions in several respects. First, the schools generally are not bound by local union contracts. Second, they are often exempt from laws unions have fought hard to institute, especially laws concerning the certification requirements for educators and the employment rights of teachers. With teachers' unions nationwide mobilizing to block charter school laws altogether, or to render them weak, one would certainly expect states with strong teachers' organizations to have no charter school laws, or to have weak ones.

Objective Educational Conditions

Another set of factors that might affect the balance of power of charter school proponents and opponents is the objective condition of public education in a state. One possibility is that in low-performing states advocates of charter schools and strong charter laws may find it advantageous to point out the existing system's dismal results. At the same time, because high-performing states are generally more reform-minded, they are more likely to consider and enact "cutting-edge" reforms such as charter school laws. To attain high levels of achievement in the past, high-performing states have had to seek out and enact innovative legislation to spur improvement. Thus their very openness to new ideas makes high-performing states more likely than low-performing states to consider, and ultimately pass, charter school legislation.

Political Culture

Finally, students of policymaking frequently suggest that states differ in their political "cultures" and that these differences produce different policies. Daniel Elazar devised a typology of state political cultures that divides states into three categories: traditionalistic, moralistic, and individualistic.[18] Individualistic cultures tend to emphasize the marketplace, favoring a limited role of government. Moralistic cultures stress "the commonwealth," fostering a more active role for the government in advancing the public good. In traditionalistic cultures, government is controlled by a relatively small elite and acts primarily to maintain existing hierarchies.

It is difficult to see how this broad category scheme could help predict outcomes on a particular policy question such as charter schools. Would one expect charter laws to emerge mostly in individualistic states, since the programs invoke various market-oriented ideas such as school-based entrepreneurialism and customer choice? Or would moralistic states be more likely to seize on the charter strategy as a way for state government to use its power to promote local school improvement? Perhaps all that one could safely predict is that states with traditionalistic cultures would shy away from charter laws altogether, and from strong charter laws in particular, in light of their disinclination to experiment with system-challenging reforms.

Perhaps a more promising line of cultural inquiry is the literature on the "innovativeness" of states, which posits that some states are more inclined than others to be on the cutting edge of reform.[19] Typically, leaders in innovation tend to be the most "developed" states, with high per capita incomes and levels of urbanization. Perhaps the differential adoption of charter schools simply reflects states' different propensities to innovate. Higher-income urban states may be more inclined to adopt charter school legislation, and strong legislation, for other reasons as well. For example, wealth and urbanness may be important underpinnings of the potential supply of school operators charter school programs demand. The wealthier states with large urban populations may place a higher value on education in general and thus be more eager to seek out methods of improvement. Urban schools, in addition, are often the most visible examples of the shortcomings of current arrangements; it may be that the case for change is more easily made in states with large urban populations. For many reasons, then, we might expect states with high incomes and large urban populations to be earlier adopters of charter laws, and of strong charter laws.

Analysis

To what extent are these "bird's-eye" political variables related to the outcomes of charter school politics in the 50 states?

Partisan Balance

First, consider party control of state legislatures. This analysis divides states into two categories: "high-GOP" (those in which Republicans controlled both houses in half or more of the years between 1991 and 1995) and "low-GOP" (those in which Republicans controlled both houses in less than half of the relevant years). But over which years should one calculate these proportions? This study examines the years 1991 (the year the first charter school law passed) through 1995. Some states, of course, passed no charter law. For these states, the relevant years are the whole period: 1991–95. For states that passed charter laws, the relevant years are all the years from 1991 to the year in which the law passed. For example, for a state that passed a charter law in 1993, the relevant years are 1991 through 1993.

Table 2-2 shows the percentages of high- and low-GOP states that adopted charter laws of some kind: 66.7 percent of states with high levels of Republican control had passed charter laws by January 1996; only 35 percent of states with low levels of GOP control had done so. And 44.4 percent of high-GOP and only 15 percent of low-GOP states had passed strong laws. These patterns suggest that high-GOP legislatures were substantially more likely to pass early and strong charter school laws.[20]

Table 2-2 contains the same sort of information for a different political variable: partisan control of the governorship. States are again divided into two categories: "high GOP" (those in which Republicans occupied the governor's office in half or more of the relevant years) and "low GOP" (those in which they did not). States with high levels of GOP control of governorships were only slightly more likely to pass charter laws (42.1 percent and 38.7 percent), an insignificant difference. By contrast, Republicans governors were relatively successful at passing strong charter laws: 36.8 percent of states with high levels of GOP control passed strong laws compared with only 9.7 percent of low-GOP states, a highly

Table 2-2. *Charter School Laws Passed by States, 1991–95*[a]

Percent

State characteristics	Passed law	Passed strong law
Control of legislature[b]		
High GOP (9)	66.7	44.4
Low GOP (40)	35.0	15.0
Control of governorship[b]		
Republican (19)	42.1	36.8
Democrat (31)	38.7	9.7
Teachers' union membership[b]		
High (25)	44.0	24.0
Low (25)	36.0	16.0
Score on NAEP 8th-grade math test[b]		
High (20)	35.0	25.0
Low (21)	52.4	23.8
Political culture[b]		
Moralistic (18)	44.4	27.8
Nonmoralistic (32)	37.5	15.6
Median income[b]		
High (25)	56.0	32.0
Low (25)	24.0	8.0
Population[b]		
High urban (25)	52.0	36.0
Low urban (25)	28.0	4.0

Sources: Council of State Governments, *State Elective Officials and Legislatures 1991–1992* (Lexington, Ky., 1991); Council of State Governments, *State Elective Officials and Legislatures 1993–1994* (Lexington, Ky., 1993); National Conference of State Legislatures, *Election Results Directory* (Denver: National Conference of State Legislatures, 1995); American Federation of Teachers, "American Federation of Teachers Membership by State," November 1998; National Association of Educators, *NEA Handbook* (Washington, 1991–92), table 2; U.S. Bureau of the Census, "Estimates of the Population of States: Annual Time Series, July 1, 1990, to July 1, 1997": http://www.census.gov/population/stimates/state/st-98-3.txt; National Assessment of Educational Progress, "Revised Mathematics Assessment Data for Grade 8," table obtained from NAEP's website: http://www.ed.gov/NCES/naep, 1996; Daniel J. Elazar, *American Federalism: A View from the States*, 3d ed. (Harper and Row, 1984), p. 137; U.S. Bureau of the Census, "Table H-8: Median Household Income by State: 1984 to 1997," published November 6, 1998: http://www.census.gov/hhes/income/histinc/h08.html; U.S. Bureau of the Census, *Statistical Abstract of the United States* (1997), table 44.

a. For a state that enacted no charter law by January 1996, these measures of partisan control are based on the years 1991–95 inclusive. For a state that enacted a charter law during this period, these measures are based on the year 1991 to the year in which the state enacted its initial charter law.

b. Numbers in parentheses represent number of states.

significant difference. In fact, eight of the ten strong statutes were signed into law by Republican governors; seven of the ten weak laws by Democratic governors.

When one considers the legislative and gubernatorial information together, the importance of Republicans becomes even more evident. No state with a Democratic governor *and* two Democratic houses of the legislature passed a strong charter school law in this period.[21] In all ten strong-law states, at least one house of the legislature or the governorship was controlled by the Republican Party when the strong law passed.

In sum, charter school laws have emerged in states with a variety of partisan configurations, a fact that lends credence to the charter strategy's reputation as a bipartisan reform. But: (1) Republican control of state legislatures appears to have created more hospitable circumstances for charter laws; (2) almost all strong charter laws have been signed by Republican governors; and (3) no state in which Democrats controlled the House, the Senate, and the governorship had put a strong charter school law on the books by January 1996.

Teachers' Organizations

Teachers' organizations are active in every state, but they are politically stronger in some states than in others. Since teachers' organizations generally have opposed charter school laws and have without exception opposed strong charter laws, one would expect states with lower union membership to be more likely to adopt charter laws and to adopt strong laws. The two major teachers' organizations whose state affiliates are involved in politics are the American Federation of Teachers and the National Education Association (NEA). The combined membership in these two organizations as a percentage of a state's population is a good measure of the potential political strength of teachers' organizations in the state. In 1991 this measure ranged from under one-half of 1 percent in some states to just over 2 percent in others, with a median of 1.1 percent.[22]

As Table 2-2 indicates, the prevalence of teachers' organizations in states bore little relation to charter school policymaking outcomes in the early to mid-1990s. Contrary to prediction, states with high teacher association membership were slightly more likely than low-membership states both to pass charter school laws and to pass strong charter school laws, but neither difference is statistically significant.

Educational Conditions

Are states with relatively high- or low-performing education systems more or less likely to pass charter school laws? To pass strong charter school laws? This analysis employs a measure of mathematics proficiency for the states' eighth-graders: their average proficiency in all content areas of the 1992 National Assessment of Educational Progress (NAEP).[23] The median state's average score on this assessment was 267.4, with state averages ranging from 246.5 to 283.4.

One can divide the states into two groups—"high-score" (those with better-than-median performance) and "low-score" those with median-or-worse performance—on each of these two measures. Table 2-2 shows how many states in each group passed charter laws and strong laws. States whose eighth-graders scored at or below the median NAEP math tests were more likely than their above-median counterparts to pass charter laws, but the difference was not statistically significant. Higher- and lower-performing states were almost equally likely to pass strong charter school laws. NAEP performance, then, does not appear to have differentiated charter-law adopters from nonadopters, or states that adopted strong laws from those that did not.[24]

"Culture"

Since many contemporary theories of state-level political culture derive from Elazar's typology, this part of the discussion begins by examining whether states with different Elazar-type cultures passed different types of charter school laws in the 1990s.[25] According to Elazar's classification, 16 states exhibited "individualistic" cultures, 18 exhibited "moralistic" cultures, and the remaining 16 exhibited "traditionalistic" cultures.[26] Table 2-2 shows that states with moralistic political cultures were more likely than other states to pass charter laws (and to pass strong ones) by January 1996, but the differences are not statistically significant.

A second notion of political culture concerns the innovativeness of states. The literature on policy innovation in the states suggests that more "modern" states are more likely to adopt innovative policies early. Two common indicators of modernity in this literature are income and urbanization. The 1990 census provides state-by-state data on both of these indicators.[27]

In general, charter school laws, and strong charter laws in particular, were more likely to be adopted in wealthier and more urban states. Higher-income states adopted charter laws at twice the rate of lower-income states. More strikingly, they adopted strong charter laws at four times the rate of lower-income states. Much the same was true for the more urban states. More urban states adopted charter school laws at just short of twice the rate of less urban states. And they enacted strong charter laws at nine times the rate of their less urban counterparts (see Table 2-2).

Combining the two variables, one finds that only three of the 20 states that were at or below the median on *both* income and urbanization adopted charter school laws, whereas 17 of the 30 that were above the median on at least one measure did so. And not a single state that was at or below the median on both income and urbanization passed a strong charter school law in this period. It appears that traditional determinants of states' "innovativeness" would have been reasonably good predictors of the adoption of charter school laws in the first half of the 1990s.

One problem with analyses such as these is that, because they examine only one factor at a time, they may fail to account for what happens when all of the factors are at play at the same time. Variables that appear unrelated to charter decisions may take on more significance when one takes account of other factors. By the same token, variables that appear important in these simple analyses may look less significant when all factors are considered. Ideally, one would include all the hypothetically important factors in a single analysis to produce more compelling results. With only 50 states to examine, however, it is difficult to conduct an analysis that includes so many independent variables.[28] A second-best approach is to conduct an analysis that includes the factors that appeared important in the above analyses (partisan control of the governorship and legislature, indicators of economic development traditionally linked to innovativeness, and political culture) along with union strength.[29] If any major problems arising from a failure to control for relevant variables exist, such a procedure should reveal it.[30]

The importance of a state's level of economic development, a traditional correlate of "innovativeness," comes through strongly in this analysis. As in the simpler analyses above, charter school laws were both more likely to emerge and to be strong in more developed states. The results are more mixed for the degree of Republican control. When other factors are taken into account, it appears that charter laws were no more likely to emerge in states with strong Republican control. However, *strong* charter laws were still much more likely to emerge in states where Republicans held the upper hand.

The most interesting finding to emerge from this more complex analysis, however, concerns the relationship between Republican control and high levels of teacher unionization: strong charter school laws were most likely to be formulated in states where Republicans held the upper hand *and* teachers' unions were strong. Fully half of the strong laws were developed in states where Republicans consistently controlled the governor's mansion and where unions were strong.

Given the apparent importance of governors in determining the strength of charter laws, how did these political actors shape the outcomes of charter school policymaking in their states? In light of the significance of at least partial Republican control of state legislatures in the passage of strong charter laws, how did the legislative process unfold when charter laws were considered? How did states' income and urbanization affect their charter school politics? And how can one account for the finding that high-union Republican states were the most fertile territory for strong charter school laws? Finding answers to these questions requires more than a bird's-eye view of the politics of charter schools. More detailed case studies of the process of charter school policymaking in several states may shed light on these questions.

3 Reaching Compromise in Four States

ALTHOUGH THE look at charter school politics in the previous chapter revealed some interesting patterns, it left critical questions unanswered. Several factors appear to have differentiated charter states from noncharter states and weak-law states from strong-law states, especially the balance of partisan power (in particular, control of the governorship) and economic characteristics associated with innovativeness. Other factors one might have expected to be important proved less so, most notably the electoral strength of educators' associations. But the purely quantitative examination of these variables did not provide much sense of how these variables served to set states apart in the early 1990s, or failed to do so. How, for example, did the nation's governors use their positions to influence the outcomes of charter debates? How exactly did income and urbanization make a difference? Why did states with strong Republican parties *and* powerful teachers' unions appear to be the most likely to pass strong charter laws?

To address these two sets of questions, this chapter presents case studies of charter school politics in four states: Colorado, Georgia, Massachusetts, and Michigan. All four enacted charter school legislation in 1993, but their

Table 3-1. *Key Provisions of Four State Charter School Laws*

Provision[a]	Colorado	Georgia	Massachusetts	Michigan
Local school boards have authority to select and oversee charter schools	Yes, but schools may appeal to state board	Yes	No	Yes, but numerous other sponsors exist
Charter schools are legally part of school districts	Yes	Yes	No	No, if chartered by other sponsor
Charter law expires on set date	Yes	No	No	No
Restrictions placed on who can obtain charter	Anyone except private, home-based, or parochial school	Yes, only existing public schools may convert	Anyone except private or parochial school	Anyone except parochial school
Scope of exemption from state law limited	No	No	Yes, most state school laws apply	Yes, most state school laws apply
Exemptions not automatic; charter school must request waivers on case-by-case basis	Yes	Yes	No, exemptions are automatic	No, exemptions are automatic
Strict limit on number of schools	Yes, 50	No	Yes, 25	No
Charter schools funded at less than per-pupil average cost	Yes	Not specified	No	No

Sources: Colorado's law is Colorado Revised Statutes (1993), secs. 22-30.5-101-114; Georgia's law is Georgia Code (1993), sec. 20-2-255; Massachusetts's law is Massachusetts Annual Laws (1993), chap. 71, sec. 89; Michigan's law is Michigan Public Act 362 (1993).

a. This table lists provisions of state charter laws as they were enacted in 1993. Some of these provisions have been changed by subsequent legislation.

four laws differed greatly. On one end of the spectrum was Georgia's law, which allowed only existing schools to convert to charter status, and only then with the approval of the local school board. On the other end was Michigan's law, which enabled a wide range of citizens to launch charter schools with the approval of any number of potential authorizers. The Massachusetts law lay close to Michigan's on the continuum of "strength," giving just about anyone the chance to start a charter school and placing no veto authority in the hands of local school committees. And Colorado's law fell near the center of the spectrum, giving local school boards a prominent role but allowing the state board of education to override local decisions. Table 3-1 provides a detailed picture of how these four laws differed across a range of important characteristics.

This analysis relies principally on three types of information. In each state, I interviewed individuals with knowledge of the political processes surrounding the passage of charter school laws: a member of governor's staff with responsibility for education; one or more legislators with a central role in charter school politics; a representative of the teachers' union or association; a representative of the school board and/or superintendents' associations; a representative of organizations advocating charter schools; and staff members of the state department of education (or equivalent) with responsibility for charter schools.

Legislative records also provide evidence of the progress of charter school bills. In each state, legislative bodies (committees and full chambers) approved numerous versions of their charter school legislation and ultimately the actual statute. Records of legislative debates were also readily available in all four states, though they are not as complete as the records of the U.S. Congress. These records made it possible to identify amendments that were proposed but rejected and to analyze votes taken on particular amendments and full bills.

Media reports about the legislative process in the four states were an additional valuable source of information.

Charter Politics: Context, Actors, Process, and Outcomes

Each of the four case studies presented here is designed to highlight the critical political factors in the passage of the four laws. I first examine the political context in which the prospect of charter schools arose. The previous chapter's quantitative analysis suggested that a state's level of economic development, measured by the income of its citizens and its level of urbanization, played a key role in its charter school politics. One possibility is that charter schools held more appeal for urban and higher-income political constituencies, and thus more urban and richer states were more likely to adopt charter laws, and to adopt strong ones. It is not clear, however, why this might have been true. Although problems of urban school districts are well publicized, educational conditions in rural areas are often just as bleak. Nationally, charter schools have sprung up in rural areas and cities alike. The link between high incomes and a preference for charter schools is even more tenuous. Low-income families are more likely than high-income families to take advantage of choices within the public system, perhaps because higher-income families already have choices about where their children attend school.[1] In short, there is no strong reason to believe that higher-income and urban citizens would have been more likely to support charter school legislation.

But a state's level of economic development might have affected charter school politics more indirectly: by influencing the broader education policy agenda in which legislatures consider charter schools. As states grow more prosperous and more urban, conflicts often arise between growing urban and suburban interests and declining rural ones. Education is one of the central battlegrounds of this conflict. Rural school districts feel the pinch of declining wealth and population, even as they watch urban and suburban school districts prosper, at least financially. Utilizing the courts or the residual political power they enjoy as a result of disproportionate representation in legislatures, rural interests nationwide have pressed for school finance reform, asking state legislatures to equalize funding between wealthier (typically urban and/or suburban) and poorer (typically rural) districts.[2] These battles over school finance can provide the occasion for the consideration of a wide range of reforms, including charter schools. Through this indirect route, then, economic development can create fertile soil for charter school politics.

Accordingly, for each state, I first examine the history of education reform immediately before the introduction of charter school legislation and other items on the education agenda contemporaneously with charter schools. In no state were charter school programs considered in isolation, so an understanding of this broader context is vital.

Second, I probe the interests and strategies of the critical actors in charter school politics. Why were they interested in charter schools in the first place, and what approach did they take to ensure that the outcome of the charter debate served those interests? Four actors receive particular attention: governors, legislators, interest groups in favor of charter schools, and traditional education interest groups, which with the exception of those in one state opposed charter schools. All four groups defined charter school politics in each state.

Third, I trace the actual process of charter policymaking in the four states. Who first proposed charter schools, and what did that initial proposal look like? As actors deployed their strategies, how did the charter legislation change? Of particular interest are the compromises charter advocates struck in an effort to secure passage of the laws. The degree of compromise determines whether a law is strong or weak.

Finally, I discuss the outcomes of the legislative process, summarizing how the charter laws enacted by each state departed from the charter "ideal."

Before proceeding to the state case studies, however, it is important to note that state-level action took place against a significant national backdrop.

National Context

As states considered charter school legislation in this period, national policy was encouraging state legislators to consider wide-ranging policy reforms in the public sector, both within education and more generally. Policymakers in state capitals, in Washington, and indeed around the globe were hearing calls to break up public sector monopolies, to reduce the level of regulation on public sector activity, to focus more on measuring results and less on accounting for inputs, to consider contracting out for more services, and to give the "customers" of government services more choice among providers.[3] Amidst widespread belief that conventional ways of doing business in the public sector had failed to deliver acceptable results, many policymakers were receptive to these new ideas. Charter school policies fell squarely within the calls to "reinvent government." In fact, in some nations with more ambitious public sector reform initiatives, charter-like programs were at the center of educational changes.[4]

Charter school programs, however, emerged as a moderate alternative to more drastic proposals for choice and competition in education. In some states, charter school laws were regarded as a compromise between staying with the status quo and establishing a system in which parents could use public money in any school of their choice, public or private. Because they kept schools within the public sector, required open enrollment and nonreligiosity, and held schools accountable to a public body for results, charter school programs were more palatable to those who feared the excesses of a full-blown choice regime.

National Actors

Politicians and other "policy entrepreneurs" at the state level drove most charter school policymaking in this period, but a national network of individuals and organizations also emerged to promote charter schools.[5] Most important were individuals, such as Ted Kolderie and Joe Nathan of Minnesota, who presented their ideas to advocates in many states, testified before legislative bodies, and spent countless hours on the phone counseling state-level charter advocates. Organizations such as the Democratic Leadership Council (DLC) and the National Governors Association (NGA) also promoted the charter idea (or variants thereof).[6] Though not advocates for charter school laws, other organizations like the Education Commission of the States (ECS) and the National Conference of State Legislatures (NCSL) helped distribute information among state policymakers about emerging legislation in the states.[7] At the same time, national entities inclined to oppose strong charter school legislation, such as the National Education Association, also participated in state-level political battles.[8] These activities, along with the national policy context, helped create the backdrop against which state-level political battles played out.

The Case of Michigan

In terms of the variables discussed in the previous chapter, circumstances in Michigan appeared auspicious for the passage of strong charter school legislation. With a Republican, John Engler, in the governor's mansion, the Senate controlled by Republicans, and the House split evenly, the partisan configuration was aligned for strong charter politics. Regarded as the heart of industrial America, Michigan was at least moderately advanced in its income and urbanization. With a median income of $29,937 and 70.5 percent of citizens living in urban areas, the state was slightly above the national median on both measures. And in Elazar's terms, Michigan exhibited a strong moralistic political culture. At the same time, Michigan was the nation's second most unionized state, with 30.4 percent of its workers in unions in 1983. The teachers' union (the Michigan Education Association, or MEA) was particularly strong, and teachers' union membership as a percentage of the population ranked seventh in the nation in 1991.[9] The Republican governor took advantage of a unique moment in the politics of education to win one of the country's strongest charter school laws. Context provided the opportunity, but gubernatorial strategy proved essential to this outcome. Unions were ineffectual despite their numerical and financial strength, both because their partisan allies lacked power and because the context militated against their effectiveness. Michigan turns out to be an excellent example of a state that produced strong charter laws with Republican control *and* high levels of unionization.

Context

In 1993, political forces converged in Michigan to produce a remarkable result: the elimination of property taxes as a source of school funding. As in many states, rural school districts found themselves in fiscally dire straits. Though Michigan was relatively prosperous, most of the prosperity was in cities and their suburbs. The state did little to equalize spending among school districts. In 1991–92, state equalization funds provided just 48.5 percent of average school spending, making Michigan one of only 14 states in which this percentage fell below 50 percent.[10] Consequently, Democrats disliked using property taxes to pay for schools because doing so generated wide disparities, leaving school systems in poorer, mostly rural districts with inadequate resources. Republicans targeted Michigan's property taxes, levied at a high rate by national standards, as part of a general drive to reduce taxes on the state's citizens. So when Democratic state senator Debbie Stabenow surprised her fellow legislators by proposing to stop funding schools with property taxes, Republicans (led by Governor John Engler) agreed.

With this action, the state's political leaders instigated a political crisis in Michigan.[11] The state's public schools faced a mammoth $6.7 billion hole in their budgets left by the departure of property taxes. Unless legislators devised a source of revenues to replace property taxes, the schools would open in 1994–95 with virtually no money. Needless to say, this deadline infused policymaking with a vital sense of urgency in the fall of 1993.

Two unique aspects of Michigan's political system intensified the crisis atmosphere. First, one of the potential strategies for replacing property tax revenues—an increase in the sales tax—would require a constitutional amendment, since Michigan's constitution limited the sales tax to 4 percent. A constitutional amendment, in turn, would require an affirmative vote in a statewide referendum. To make sure that the referendum happened in time to generate revenues for the 1994–95 school year, legislators needed to act quickly. Second, laws passed in Michigan cannot take effect until the following calendar year unless a super-majority authorizes a law to take "immediate effect." Since in the highly contested politics of school finance reform a super-majority was exceedingly unlikely, lawmakers felt the need to pass a package of reforms before the end of calendar year 1993 so that they would take effect in time for the start of school in the fall of 1994. Together, these factors led legislators and the governor to impose a December 31, 1993, deadline on themselves for addressing Michigan's school funding crisis.[12]

Another element in Michigan's political context was a movement, led by the nonprofit TEACH Michigan, to institute a system of vouchers that would allow families to spend tax dollars in private and parochial schools. Michigan's constitution flatly prohibits such a program through the so-called Parochiaid Amendment, but TEACH Michigan director Paul DeWeese was mobilizing support for a referendum to amend that provision.[13] Although such a referendum had no chance of passing in the near future, the mere possibility had aroused concern among opponents.

Actors

Democratic legislator Stabenow made the opening move by proposing to eliminate the property tax, but Republican governor Engler quickly seized the initiative. According to his advisers and press reports at the time, his strategy was straightforward: make substantial education reform a condition of finance reform. In October 1993, Engler delivered an address before the state legislature, accompanied by a document entitled "Our Kids Deserve Better" outlining his proposals for education reform.[14] "Let's tear down the Berlin Wall of separation that has held kids hostage to one school district," Engler intoned. "It is time to tear down the wall! Our families want their freedom! And they want it now!"[15] Engler's proposals spanned a wide array of educational issues. The package included:

—major changes to the state's tax code;
—an overhaul of school finance, centered on a state-funded "foundation grant" program to ensure that all districts had adequate resources;
—gubernatorial appointment of the state school superintendent;
—a study of school district consolidation;
—major changes in school labor law, including abolishing tenure and granting teachers the right *not* to join a union;
—a state-mandated core curriculum and statewide system of "report cards" to measure student progress;
—inter- and intradistrict public school choice.

Engler also proposed a charter school program far more ambitious than any other state had yet attempted. Most striking, the range of organizations authorized to approve charter schools was extremely wide. In addition to local school boards, intermediate school boards, and the state board of education, the bill empowered state university and community college boards of trustees, a newly created state charter school authority, and "any other public body other than a charter public school."[16] A "public body" was defined broadly as:

> a state officer, agency, department, division, bureau, board, commission, council, authority, or other body in the executive, judicial, or legislative branch of the state government; a county, city, township, village, regional governing body, or council, special district, or municipal corporation, or a board, department, commission, council, or agency thereof; or any other body created by state or local government.[17]

In addition, the bill provided for the legal independence of charter schools, automatic waivers of state laws, no cap on the number of charter schools in the state, and full per-pupil funding.

Ordinarily, perhaps, such an expansive proposal would have been declared dead on arrival in the legislature, especially when combined with such a wide-ranging set of additional reforms. But in 1993, political conditions rendered Engler's package much more feasible. In addition to the urgency imposed by the financial crisis, the partisan balance in the state legislature also worked in Engler's favor. Republicans controlled the Senate with a five-member advantage, 22 to 16. The House was evenly split, with 55 Democrats and 55 Republicans. It was the first time in 24 years that Democrats had held anything less than outright control of the House.[18] If most Republicans followed Engler's lead, the defection of a handful of Democrats would open the door for even the most radical of Engler's proposals.

Engler also enjoyed the support of some important interest groups. One was TEACH Michigan, the small organization mentioned above that was brewing a campaign for school vouchers. TEACH Michigan knew that vouchers would be a long time coming because they required an amendment to the state constitution. So in 1993 the organization turned its focus to charter schools, hiring attorney Richard McClellan to draft a proposal. The TEACH Michigan draft served as the basis for the governor's eventual bill. The organization's director, Paul DeWeese, conducted an active campaign to distribute newsletters and op-ed pieces and spoke widely to generate support for the plan.[19] Though influential in policy circles, TEACH Michigan lacked the electoral muscle to push its proposal through. For that, Engler turned to business organizations. As early as August, before Engler had even made his pitch, the Michigan Manufacturers' Association came out in support of what would become Engler's core strategy: insisting on quality reforms as a condition of finance reform.[20] As the fall wore on, business groups formed the Coalition for Better Schools in 1993 to press for a whole range of school reforms, including charters.[21] The coalition sent top corporate executives to roam the halls of the state legislature promoting Engler's agenda.[22]

Arrayed against the Engler proposal, however, were a number of education organizations known in Michigan for their power in the state legislature. At the center of the opposition was the Michigan Education Association, the state's National Education Association affiliate. The MEA's more than 125,000 members made it a formidable voice in state politics in sheer electoral terms. The MEA's substantial base also made it a top contributor to political campaigns. The organization collected campaign funds from members through a "reverse check-off" procedure in which each member contributed one dollar per month unless he or she specifically chose not to. No Michigan political action committee donated more money to state candidates in 1991–92 than the MEA's, which gave more than seven times as much money to Democratic candidates as the largest contributor to Republican candidates provided for GOP hopefuls. Indeed, the MEA political action committee accounted for a quarter of all funds contributed by special interests to Democratic candidates in those years. One anonymous insider told the *Detroit Free Press*: "While the other unions talk big, the MEA backs it up with the dollars. In many respects, they are the Democratic Party."[23] If votes and money were not enough, the MEA could also point to the fact that fully a quarter of the state legislators (37 of 148) had been schoolteachers before their election.[24]

In Michigan, an internal MEA memo listed opposition to charter schools as one of 23 points guiding the organization's legislative strategy in fall 1993.[25] When Governor Engler unveiled his school-reform plan, with its robust charter school provision, the MEA immediately denounced the idea and continued to do so throughout the fall, with one official calling the plan "a gimmick that doesn't address the real issue of quality public education."[26] On the whole range of school-reform issues confronting Michigan that fall, the MEA orchestrated a massive lobbying campaign, hiring ten additional lobbyists, running television ads, seeking to raise a $10 million war chest, and sending two teachers a day to Lansing (the capital) from each legislative district.[27] Interviews with MEA officials confirm the organization's outright opposition to the plan.[28]

Several other organizations joined the MEA in opposition to the charter proposal (and most other aspects of the governor's plan). The smaller teachers' union, the AFT-affiliated Michigan Federation of Teachers, led its 25,000 members in opposing the plan.[29] The Michigan Association of School Administrators also stood in opposition.[30] The Michigan Association of School Boards (MASB) expressed support for a charter program that would leave chartering decisions solely to local school boards. But since Engler's idea of charter schools spread that authority so widely, MASB joined the other organizations in speaking against the proposal.[31]

Despite these organizations' history of political strength in Michigan (and especially that of the MEA), the opponents of charter schools were not in a strong position to press their claims in 1993, for several reasons. First, the MEA and its allies wielded most of their political power through the Democratic Party. Almost all of the MEA's substantial political war chest, for example, went to support Democratic candidates. To the extent that the MEA could hope to capitalize on this "investment" to win votes in the legislature, it could mostly hope to win Democratic votes. Even if the MEA's money talked in Michigan politics, then, it did not have much to say to Republicans. In 1993, however, winning Democratic votes was not enough. With a Republican governor, Republicans in control of the Senate, and Republicans sharing a joint speakership based on the even party split in the House, the MEA and its allies were ill-positioned to win on issues of importance.

Second, these organizations' top priority in 1993 was finance reform.[32] With property taxes eliminated as a source of funds for schooling, it was imperative that the state find some alternative source of revenue. With proponents of reform, including charter schools, holding the balance of power in state politics, it seemed inevitable that these education interest groups would have to compromise on reform in order to win approval of a financing scheme.

Third, charter schools were just one of several reforms that these organizations felt a need to fight in 1993. Teachers' associations, for example, faced the potential abolition of tenure and state legislation that would allow schoolteachers to opt out of union membership. The school board and school administrator associations faced the possibility of moves to consolidate school districts, effectively shutting down some of their members' operations. All of these groups also worried about the threat of a sweeping interdistrict school choice program. Under these circumstances, organizations could only devote so much time to fighting charter legislation specifically. As one interest group lobbyist remarked in an interview, "When you look at a little bill over here on charters, it was so small you couldn't give it the time." Another called the charter bill "kind of a footnote."

Fourth, all of this politicking took place amidst the "crisis atmosphere" of 1993, in which the legislature had a December 31 deadline to pass finance and education reform.[33] Perhaps with an extended time frame, tactics of delay could have mitigated some of the unfavorable political circumstances in which the educational organizations found themselves. But with the rush to closure, deals had to be struck.

Finally, the teachers' unions' strength paradoxically became a liability in light of these other factors. Republicans, led by Governor Engler, were able to make unions the enemy, raising the specter of a self-interested lobby bent on blocking popular reforms to maintain its own status, even at the expense of children. The MEA's very strength became part of the governor's argument for change.

Process

Republican legislators introduced two separate but identical bills, House Bill 5124 by Representative William Bryant and Senate Bill 896 by Senator Richard Posthumus. The Senate Education Committee was the first to take up the legislation. Even though Republicans held the majority on the committee (and in the Senate), the range of potential approving authorities proposed by Governor Engler was far too broad to gain acceptance. The committee eliminated the "other public bodies" provision.[34] On the Senate floor, numerous amendments were proposed, but few were of major importance. The most significant was to require charter schools to follow the state constitution and other strictures with regard to church-state relations; it passed without dissent.

The bill passed on November 2 much as the committee had approved it.[35] It should be noted that even with the "public bodies" provision gone, the bill still provided a broad range of chartering authorities. Relative to Engler's proposal, the elimination of "other public bodies" was a compromise; relative to other states' laws, Michigan's range of authorizers was still wide.[36] Thus, not surprisingly given the Senate's partisan makeup, the Senate passed a very uncompromised charter bill. But support for it was not overwhelming. In the first vote on the bill a majority of senators failed to vote yes. When it later passed, it did so by a single vote.

Shortly thereafter, though, charter proponents began to worry that the bill's language would not pass constitutional muster. As noted above, Michigan's constitution flatly prohibits state aid to private schools, and some legal experts believed that as the law was written charter schools could be construed as private schools. Attorney McClellan was enlisted to redraft the legislation to respond to these concerns. Since the bill was then up for grabs, opponents of charter legislation also entered the negotiations in an effort to pull the legislation back from the strong language adopted by the Senate. These talks culminated in a marathon negotiating session in early December in which a compromise was hammered out. Legislators, their aides, the governor's staff, and McClellan were the primary direct participants, but interest group representatives were consulted at key points in the discussions.[37]

Though all of this rewriting and negotiation took place behind closed doors, it is possible to obtain a sense of the issues Democrats raised by tracing the House debate over its own charter legislation, House Bill 5124.[38] In the evenly split House, charter proponents needed to gain at least some Democratic support in order to pass the legislation. The result was a compromise. Democrats on the House Education Committee took aim at the broad range of sponsors contemplated in the Senate, approving a bill that dropped the state board of education and the to-be-created charter school authority from the list of eligible charter school authorizers. This move left the boards of local school districts, intermediate school districts, state universities, and community colleges with the power to charter (still an expansive list by national standards).[39] The committee also required charter schools to apply for waivers on a case-by-case basis and to support their requests with research, and it placed strict limits on the waivers schools could request. For example, it did not allow schools to request a waiver of the requirement to hire certified teachers.[40] Press reports suggested the committee's actions had broken the impasse over charter schools, forging a compromise sufficient to win the approval of the full House.[41]

In the November 29, 1993, debate on the House floor, two Republican representatives, eager for a more permissive bill, proposed amendment after amendment that would have reversed compromises forged in Senate and House committees. Democrats, generally supportive of the compromises, voted against these proposals in unity. And a group of moderate Republicans, eager to preserve a compromise that would win House approval, joined their colleagues across the aisle to uphold committee compromises. For example, 17 Republicans sided with 44 Democrats to block a bid supported by 37 Republicans to exempt charter schools from teacher certification requirements. Republicans were almost evenly split on a motion to authorize the state board of education to approve charter schools (27 for, 25 against).

Many of the changes made by the House, in fact, appeared in the compromise hammered out in the back room in early December. Most notably, this agreement limited authorizing power to the boards of local districts, intermediate districts, state universities, and community colleges, just as the House had done. While it imposed most public school law on charter schools, including teacher certification requirements, it did not require schools to obtain waivers case by case.

Strangely, even though negotiators had reached agreement on these matters and planned to reconsider Senate Bill 896, the Senate enacted House Bill 5124 on December 10. Since that bill did not contain a full response to the constitutional questions that had been raised, however, both the Senate and the House also then passed Senate Bill 896, which superseded the House bill. The Senate version passed both houses with minimal debate and with overwhelming majorities (31 to 3 in the Senate; 97 to 2 in the House).

Summary of Outcomes

Michigan's 1993 charter law contained fewer compromises than the laws of other states. It enabled a wide range of groups to apply for charter status; allowed applicants to approach a variety of potential authorizers—not just the boards of local school districts, but those of intermediate school districts, community colleges, and public universities as well; and set no cap on the number of charter schools. The primary compromise in Michigan was to subject charter schools to virtually all state school law.

The Case of Massachusetts

Political circumstances on the eve of consideration of charter legislation were ambiguous in Massachusetts. On the one hand, Massachusetts had a Republican governor and strong advocate of school reform in William Weld. And the state's economic development ranked it among the most advanced, with a median income of $36,247 and 84.3 percent of its citizens residing in urban areas. On the other hand, Democrats controlled both houses of the legislature, and a relatively high proportion of the state's population belonged to teachers' associations.[42] In Elazar's terms, Massachusetts's political culture was individualistic. But despite its differences with Michigan, Massachusetts followed a similar course. As in Michigan, the Republican governor exploited a unique political context to press for a relatively strong charter law. As in Michigan, ordinarily strong unions were rendered powerless, in part by the context in which charters were debated. Unlike in Michigan, though, many Democratic leaders joined Republicans in backing charter reform, further weakening the hand of the teachers' union.

Context

It would not be a stretch to argue that Massachusetts's journey toward a charter school law began 15 years before the law's enactment. In 1978 several school committees in the commonwealth's poorer (mostly rural) school districts filed suit against then governor Michael Dukakis, alleging that the state's property-tax-based system of school finance denied poor children equal access to education. Citing the Massachusetts constitution's requirement that the state "cherish the interests of literature and science," the plaintiffs in *Webby* v. *Dukakis* argued that state government had an obligation to ensure that school districts, regardless of their wealth, had adequate funding to provide public education for their children. Joined by a host of education interest groups, the plaintiffs formed the Council for Fair School Finance to press their claim. Finance reform legislation in 1985 put the case on temporary hold by providing some state funding for poor districts, but the lawsuit was far from over. When Massachusetts voters passed Proposition 2½, limiting the annual growth in property tax levies to 2.5 percent, they placed school districts under severe financial stress, especially rural districts with small tax bases.[43] By 1990 the Council for Fair School Finance had revived its lawsuit, which would eventually be called *McDuffy* v. *Robertson*.[44] In 1991–92, state equalization funds provided just 40.6 percent of average school spending, the third lowest percentage in the nation.[45]

Events in 1991 heightened the sense of crisis surrounding school finance in Massachusetts. Early in the year the Massachusetts Business Alliance for Education (MBAE) issued a call for reform of the state's educational system. Most strikingly, the business group called for the state to guarantee a "foundation" level of per-pupil resources in each district, even if the district's property tax revenues were insufficient. At the same time, MBAE argued, the state should revamp key aspects of education policy: creating statewide standards and assessments, holding schools and districts accountable for performance, placing more authority at the school level, limiting the tenure rights of teachers, and other measures.[46] Calls for reform gained more momentum when New Jersey's highest court struck down that state's system of school finance on much the same grounds that the Massachusetts plaintiffs were pressing.[47] And some poor school districts saw even more dire financial straits ahead with the implementation of the state's new school choice plan, through which funding would follow students to the districts of their choice.[48]

In short, the political context in 1991 favored some kind of major school reform in Massachusetts. The precise shape of the reform package, however, and the place of charter schools in it, would depend on actions taken by the key policy actors over the next two years.

Actors

Republican governor William Weld came into office calling for a major overhaul in the way the state of Massachusetts did business. In the fall of 1991, on the heels of President George Bush's national education summit with the governors, Weld unveiled his "Massachusetts 2000" plan for overhauling the state's school system. Though the *Boston Globe* called the plan a "skimpy draft" full of "sketchy proposals," it did outline a series of quality reforms in public education very similar to the blueprint put forward by the Massachusetts Business Alliance for Education.[49] Among other measures, Weld's plan aimed to impose statewide standards and tests, eliminate tenure for teachers, and expand school choice. Weld also acknowledged the need for more funding for schools in poorer districts. But he staked out two positions that turned out to be critical in the debate. First, having campaigned on a pledge of "no new taxes," Weld insisted that the state obtain any new funding for schools by trimming expenses in other parts of the state budget. Second, and even more vital for this discussion, Weld made clear that he would not accept any increases in school funding that were not part of a broader package of quality reforms. In effect, like Governor Engler in Michigan, Weld told advocates of finance reform that he would go along with their spending plans only if they agreed to his school reforms. As one of his aides told the press: "We are going to earmark local aid to schools. The Governor wants reform, but he did not want to pour money into a bad system."[50]

In the legislature, the Democratic Party enjoyed margins in both houses, dominating the Senate 26 to 14 and the House 121 to 38 in 1991. With a Republican in the governor's mansion, the state looked set for extreme partisan conflict over education reform. In November of 1991, however, the Democratic heads of the legislative education committees, Representative Mark Roosevelt and Senator Thomas Birmingham, unveiled the Educational Excellence and Accountability Act. With the finance crisis looming, the bill contained provisions to increase state aid to schools in an effort to help the lower-spending districts. But the plan also featured numerous quality reforms that closely mirrored the governor's proposals. "There is a distinct bipartisan unity to the package," wrote the *Boston Globe*, "with the two Democratic legislators promoting school choice, generally regarded as a conservative's answer to school reform, and public funding of autonomous [charter] schools, independent of public school systems. It is widely agreed that this is a climate in which change can happen."[51] The proposal eliminated tenure; created a career ladder for teachers; capped school administrative expenses at 15 percent of school budgets; transferred hiring and firing authority from school committees to principals; set statewide standards and assessments; expanded the state's school choice program; authorized charter schools; and created a new state agency to conduct "educational audits" of schools, issue "report cards," and close down or seize "educationally bankrupt" schools.[52]

In this stroke, leading Democrats joined Governor Weld in one of his key strategic moves: linking finance reform with quality reform. Not only that, but they agreed on the core elements of the policy changes that were needed. Where the two sides parted ways was over money: how much more to spend and where to get the money. As described below, that disagreement would ultimately stall reform for more than a year. But the early agreement between Democratic legislative leaders and the Republican governor on both the need for quality reform and its fundamental shape was notable and quite important to the fate of charter legislation in Massachusetts. How did this remarkable agreement come about? Why were Democrats, in particular, willing to sign on to a plan also endorsed by the Republican governor? One factor appears to have been the national policy context. Democratic leaders in Massachusetts were convinced that traditional ways of doing things in government were unlikely to be effective. But they were also motivated by a practical calculation that only a package that combined quality and finance reform would pass muster politically.

Also active in educational politics were organizations of various types. As noted above, the Massachusetts Business Alliance for Education played a vital role in forging consensus between Democrats and Republicans. The organization's reform blueprint, issued earlier in 1991, formed the basis for the plans put forward by both Governor Weld and the Democrats. The more general organization representing the state's large corporations, the Massachusetts Business Roundtable, moved to back the reform package in early 1992.[53] Other support for many of the reforms came from a conservative think tank, the Pioneer Institute. Pioneer published a book by Steven F. Wilson in 1992, entitled *Reinventing the Schools: A Radical Plan for Boston*.[54] Though the volume focused on the state's largest school system, many of its proposals and arguments provided support for key provisions of the emergent consensus on statewide reform. In particular, Wilson made a charter-like proposal for school change: "A plan for the schools must . . . extend an invitation for school entrepreneurs to step forward from the ranks of Boston's teachers, as well as business people and others outside the schools, and put them in charge. Each such leader will identify the specific ideals for which his school stands and establish the best means to achieve them."[55]

Traditional public education interest groups—associations of teachers, school committees, and superintendents—faced a difficult strategic choice in 1991. On the one hand, they favored finance reform, especially if it included (as both the Weld and legislative plans did) an overall increase in funding for schools. On the other hand, many of the proposed quality reforms attacked long-held positions of these organizations. Teachers' unions stood to lose ground if seniority systems were weakened or tenure eliminated. School committees and superintendents feared the loss of hiring and firing power to principals. All were wary of the emphasis on standards and assessments and of proposed expansions in the state's school choice program. And charter schools posed threats to all of them, since they were to be completely independent of school committees, and thus of superintendents and collective bargaining agreements as well. Because money would follow students to charter schools, all of these groups faced the prospect of a diminished pie of resources to divide.

Teachers' unions led the opposition to the charter proposal. As in many states, most Massachusetts teachers belonged to one of two unions: the Massachusetts Teachers' Association (MTA), the 65,000-member affiliate of the National Education Association; and the Massachusetts Federation of Teachers (MFT), the smaller, 15,000-member affiliate of the American Federation of Teachers. Although both expressed opposition to the charter provisions of the education reform package, the MTA was particularly outspoken. MTA president Roseanne Bacon called it "one of the most dangerous things in this plan.[56] In an interview, MTA spokesperson Steve Wollmer confirmed the MTA's outright opposition to any inclusion of charters in the reform package. Prominent school committees (like Boston's) and the Massachusetts Association of School Committees (MASC) also opposed the charter idea, though they kept a lower profile.[57]

These organizations, particularly the MTA, had a reputation for power in the state legislature. In a 1987 survey of legislators and their aides, legislators rated organized labor the state's most influential lobbying force. Aides said labor tied with business organizations for the top ranking. The MTA tied with two other groups in receiving the most mentions from both legislators and aides as a powerful lobby.[58]

As in Michigan, however, the overall political context constrained the degree to which education interest groups could successfully oppose charter schools, in three key respects. First, the early consensus between Republican governor Weld and the Democratic leadership in the legislature shifted the political center of gravity in the state sharply toward a more "radical" reform agenda, including charters. Education groups that had traditionally counted on Democrats to back their interests suddenly found themselves fighting against an emerging bipartisan consensus.[59] Second, the reform agenda included much more than just charters. Education groups faced a major retrenchment in some of their central powers and vital policy positions. As an interview with the MTA's Wollmer confirmed, education groups could not afford to devote substantial attention to blocking the charter legislation. Finally, the "carrot" of finance reform—and the likelihood that finance reform would not happen without substantial quality reform—made these groups willing to consider compromises they would never have entertained under normal circumstances. In fact, in March of 1992, the two teachers' organizations took an unprecedented step, joining together in announcing a package of reforms both organizations would champion. While not as wide-ranging or thoroughgoing as either the Weld or Democratic plans, the unions' proposals did call for streamlining the dismissal process for teachers, among other reforms.[60] That the unions would forward such a plan was testament to the unique political circumstances in 1991–92.

Process

With strong bipartisan unity and potential opponents somewhat hamstrung, the prospects seemed ripe in late 1991 for swift action. But the Massachusetts Education Reform Act did not receive Governor Weld's signature until June of 1993. The intervening year and a half featured seemingly endless negotiations and numerous false starts. Although many issues rose to the surface, how much more to spend on schools and where to get the money dominated the discussions for most of 1992 and 1993. Democratic and business leaders were willing to raise taxes and to allow localities to circumvent (temporarily) Proposition 2½ tax limits in order to bring school spending up to the mark; Weld ruled out new taxes and changes to Proposition 2½.[61] Negotiations dragged on through the spring. When the prospects looked bleak, the MTA threatened a teachers' strike if political leaders could not agree on a finance package for the following fall.[62] Fed up himself with the slow progress, Weld broke ranks in June with the legislative leadership and proposed his own legislation. Also during the summer, business leaders split. The MBAE (the initial driving force behind the widely accepted reform plan) criticized Weld for refusing to make concessions on taxes; other business people, led by State Street Bank chairman William S. Edgerly, backed Weld.[63] Rejecting Weld's plan, legislators passed a budget that included new funding for schools, but no quality reforms. Weld vetoed the line item, but the heavily Democratic legislature overrode him.[64] The momentum behind reform, however, was not dead. The new funding was small and did not revamp the system of school finance. So in December of 1992, when the state's Supreme Judicial Court agreed to take the *McDuffy* v. *Robertson* school finance case, legislators went back to the drawing board on reform, and the Joint Committee on Education produced the Education Reform Act in January of 1993.

Over the ensuing months, Weld had proposed a cap of five charter schools per district (amounting to nearly 2,000 across the Commonwealth), but the Education Committee recommended a statewide cap of 24. Whereas Weld had placed authority over charter schools in the hands of the board of education, the Democrats favored giving that authority to the state's secretary of education, an appointee of the governor.[65] But both the Republican governor and the Democratic legislative committee agreed that some state entity, not local school committees, should take the helm. The House Ways and Means Committee amended the bill further, moving the cap up a notch to 25 and reinstating the state board of education's role.[66] On the House floor, bipartisan majorities rebuffed attempts to weaken the bill. One proposal to shift authority over charter schools to local school committees failed on a 51 to 105 vote. Another, which would have required the state, rather than local districts, to pay for charter schools, also failed. The bill that emerged from the House, then, was a strong one: it capped the number of charter schools but left them independent from local school committees and granted them broad exemptions from state law.[67]

The bill's next stop was the Senate Ways and Means Committee, which made several changes, three of which were particularly significant. First, the committee dropped the cap altogether. Second, it shifted authority back (again) to the secretary of education. Third, it specified more clearly charter schools' legal powers—and restrictions on those powers. The bill made clear that charter schools were exempt from the main state laws concerning the hiring and firing of teachers. But it also made clear that charter schools were subject to the state's bilingual education laws, which had gone unmentioned in previous versions.[68] On the floor, senators defeated an amendment that would have required charter applicants to reach agreement with district collective bargaining units on exemptions from teacher contracts. They also expanded the range of potential charter-seekers to include businesses.[69]

The issue of the cap became the critical negotiating point, with senators arguing for unlimited charters and House members promoting a cap. Ultimately, lawmakers agreed on a cap of 25. The rest of the provisions followed the Senate's version, giving sole authority over charter schools to the secretary of education.[70]

For charter schools to become law, the entire Education Reform Act of 1993 had to pass, from teacher tenure to school choice to school finance. Finally, though, in June of 1993, legislators agreed on a package and Governor Weld, with some reluctance, signed the bill into law.

Summary of Outcomes

The charter law that passed in Massachusetts contained a blend of strong and weak provisions. On the strong side, the law allowed virtually any entity to organize a charter school (though not existing private schools); gave local school committees no power to block approval of charter schools or meddle in their affairs once chartered; and exempted charter schools from some important state laws on personnel. On the weak side, the law placed strict caps on the number of students and schools and subjected charter schools to most state education law.

The Case of Colorado

Colorado's political configuration on the eve of consideration of charter legislation was in some ways the opposite of that in Massachusetts: Colorado had a Democratic governor, two Republican houses of the legislature, a relatively low level of teacher unionization, and a moralistic political culture.[71] Like Massachusetts, though, Colorado had a high median income ($30,733) and a large proportion of city residents (82.4 percent). All in all, circumstances appeared favorable for strong charter legislation. But whereas Republican governors in Massachusetts and Michigan took advantage of policy crises to win strong charter laws, Colorado's Democratic governor effected a more moderate outcome in a context decidedly lacking in crisis.

Context

As in Michigan and Massachusetts, events before 1993 set the stage for charter school legislation in Colorado. In contrast to Michigan and Massachusetts, by 1993 Colorado had already taken great strides in addressing disparities in spending between school districts. In 1991–92, state equalization funds accounted for 76.2 percent of average school funding, the twelfth highest percentage in the country and much higher than Michigan's 48.5 percent and Massachusetts's 40.6 percent.[72] As in Massachusetts and Michigan, poorer rural districts pressed the state for school funding as their wealth and population dwindled. But Colorado's battle over school funding equity had already taken place by 1993. The 1988 Public School Finance Act had equalized spending and incorporated a range of quality reforms.[73]

In addition, four political decisions in 1992—one in the legislature and three at the ballot box—generated the context into which charter schools emerged the following year. The legislative decision was the disposition of the Independent School District Act, proposed by Republican senator William Owens and Democratic representative John Irwin. Inspired by the United Kingdom's recent reform that allowed local schools to secede from their local school districts, the legislators proposed the establishment of a new statewide school district. New schools would be able to form and apply for membership in the district; existing schools, like their British counterparts, would be able to join the new statewide jurisdiction. Students from anywhere in the state would be eligible to attend these independent schools, and their funding would follow them. The bill did not use the term "charter schools," but the scheme it proposed was indistinguishable from the charter concept.[74]

The bill languished in the Senate Education Committee. According to the bill's Republican sponsor, one of the critical reasons the bill failed was that it allowed schools to completely bypass their elected local school boards.[75] Colorado has a relatively strong tradition of local control of schools. Its constitution, for example, explicitly forbids the state to select a state list of textbooks.[76] Even though Republicans controlled both houses of the legislature, the state's policymakers were unwilling to enact a law that represented such a major departure from the state's tradition of local control.[77] This initial foray into charter-like territory, though, sowed the seeds for Colorado's unique version of charter school legislation the following year.

At the ballot box, Colorado voters rejected two referendums in 1992 with ramifications for the context of education policymaking in 1993. First, they voted down a proposition that would have instituted a statewide voucher program. Second, they defeated Amendment 6, which would have raised the sales tax to provide more funds for education. Colorado policymakers credit both of these votes with helping usher in charter legislation. Though the voucher initiative failed by a wide margin, it raised the prospect of a substantial threat to public education in the state. With proponents vowing to try again, defenders of public education regarded the vote as a wake-up call, suggesting the need for less radical, but significant, reform of the public schools. The defeat of the proposed sales tax hike similarly alarmed public school advocates and sent a signal that the public's confidence in the status quo was weak. The financial crisis predicted by proponents of the tax increase never materialized, but reform-minded legislators believed the defeat of the tax increase galvanized support for change in general and for charter schools in particular. According to Senator Owen, who had proposed the Independent Public School Act: "Charter schools is something I don't think would have passed except for the defeat of Amendment 6."[78]

At the same time, voters narrowed the Republican margin in the state legislature. Before the 1992 elections, Republicans enjoyed an 11-vote majority in both the Senate and the House. In 1992 the Democrats narrowed the advantage to three in both bodies.[79] With Democratic governor Roy Romer halfway through his second term, Democrats looked forward to a 1993 legislative session with considerably more political power than they held in 1992.

Unlike Michigan and Massachusetts, then, Colorado's legislature took up a relatively uncrowded education agenda in 1993. It considered adopting statewide guidelines for content-based standards and assessments as well as interdistrict school choice, but charter schools quickly emerged as one of the primary items for consideration.[80]

Actors

As in Massachusetts and Michigan, Colorado's governor exerted a great deal of influence over education policymaking. In contrast to his Republican counterparts to the east, however, Democrat Romer did not launch an all-out reform barrage in 1993. According to his education policy adviser, Romer regarded the state's tradition of local, democratic control of schooling as sacred.[81] Accordingly, he had led the fight against the voucher initiative in 1992 and had opposed the Independent School District Act.[82] Romer viewed himself as an education reformer; he was associated with the moderate Democratic Leadership Council, an early promoter of charter schools. He proposed reforms, though, that left the basic system of school governance in place, with most power in the hands of elected local school districts. For example, his standards and assessment bill authorized the state department of education to develop "model" benchmarks and tests but allowed local districts to adopt their own policies based on these models.

Romer's approach to charter schools followed this orientation as well. Though he opposed the Independent School District Act, which bypassed local school districts, he let it be known in early 1993 that he would back a charter school bill that granted sufficient authority to local school districts. Whereas Michigan's Engler proposed a charter bill that would have authorized any public body to approve charter schools, and Massachusetts's Weld put forth a proposal in which only a state entity could authorize charters, Romer wanted all charter applicants to approach their school districts first.[83]

In the legislature, charter backer and Republican senator Owens headed the Education Committee. Having failed to pass his Independent School District Act the previous year, Owens was ready to press for a compromise bill capable of winning the support of the governor, legislative Democrats, and moderate Republicans in the more balanced legislature. To win this broad support, Owens believed, the bill would have to require charter applicants to approach their local school boards for approval first. To maintain the interest of Owens and other Republicans, though, the compromise would need to contain some mechanism for rejected charter applicants to appeal to a higher authority, like the state board of education.[84] These general terms were sufficient to satisfy Governor Romer and House minority leader Peggy Kerns, a DLC-oriented Democrat who signed on early as a cosponsor of charter legislation.

Political leaders received support from a unique collection of interest groups. As in Michigan and Massachusetts, much of this backing came from predictable sources: conservative advocacy groups and business organizations. The Independence Institute, for example, had been agitating for years for more school choice in Colorado, and this conservative think tank lined up enthusiastically behind charter legislation.[85] Small businesses, represented by the National Federation of Independent Businesses/Colorado, also came out in favor of charter schools.[86] And the broad-based Colorado Association of Commerce and Industry testified on behalf of the idea at legislative hearings on charter legislation.[87] At the same time, though, the charter idea received support from organizations not usually associated with conservative or business causes. For example, both Barbara O'Brien of the child advocacy organization Colorado Children's Campaign and Rex Brown of the Denver-based think tank Education Commission of the States testified on behalf of charters at House and Senate hearings.[88]

As in the other states in this study, though, education interest groups expressed their disapproval of the charter concept early on. Local school systems and an "Educational Coalition" consisting of groups like the NEA-affiliated Colorado Education Association (CEA), the Colorado Association of School Executives, the Colorado PTA, and the Colorado Association of School Boards (CASB) testified against charter schools from the outset at both House and Senate hearings.[89] The CEA's Dan Morris argued that charter schools "could siphon off funds from a public school system that is in crisis because of funding"; would lower educational standards by bringing unlicensed educators into the classroom; and could "encourage elite enclaves and foster segregation." Morris suggested that the CEA and its allies did not oppose charter schools per se, but the conditions they asked legislators to impose (local school board veto over charter approval, teacher veto power over charter approval, no adverse financial consequences for school districts) would have rendered a charter bill essentially meaningless.[90] CASB too opposed any charter bill that did not allow local school boards to veto charter proposals. As CASB executive director Randy Quinn wrote after the legislation passed: "Make no mistake about it: the Colorado Association of School Boards opposed the bill creating charter schools. . . . CASB worked vigorously before and during the legislative session to shape charter schools into a bill that would be more acceptable to local school board members. When that did not happen, we worked just as vigorously to kill the bill."[91] Quinn added in an interview: "Our preference is to try to maintain as much local authority as we can. There are dollars at stake here."[92]

Education interest and labor groups, however, had a reputation for weakness in Colorado. Though in one study the AFL-CIO and CEA ranked second and third in their political contributions, 100 percent and

84 percent of their funding respectively went to Democratic candidates, the long-standing underdogs in Colorado legislative politics. Analyses of Colorado interest group activity have generally found business groups to be dominant.[93]

Process

In early 1993 legislators introduced charter legislation with the backing of Republican senator Owens, Democratic House minority leader Kerns, and Governor Romer. As suggested above, the bill struck a critical compromise, requiring charter school organizers to go first to their local school boards for approval. Only after rejection there could they approach a statewide entity, the state board of education, with an appeal.[94]

This compromise was sufficient to gain some support, but not enough to obtain the votes required for passage or to defuse interest group opposition to the bill. The principal effect of the initial compromise was to secure the backing of Governor Romer, who rallied Democrats in support of the plan. As one report on charter schools in Colorado noted two years later: "The bill appeared dead several times and was resuscitated only through the energetic leadership of Governor Roy Romer."[95]

Though resuscitated, the bill went through numerous revisions. In the Senate Education Committee, which marked up the bill in February 1993, legislators made a series of amendments that strengthened the authority of local boards. They made clear that charter schools would be legally part of local school districts, that a local board could revoke or refuse to renew a charter if it determined the school was not in the best interests of the district's pupils, that school boards could negotiate the amount of funding a charter school would receive, and that an appeal had to meet a higher standard of review for the state board to overturn a local decision.[96] The committee also imposed three significant new provisions: it capped the number of charter schools at eight per congressional district, required charter schools to seek waivers from state rules on a case-by-case basis, and ordered the law to expire in 1998.[97] On the Senate floor, opponents of the bill tried to impose an additional compromise at the behest of education interest groups: eliminating the possibility of appeal to the state board. An amendment to do so failed on the floor by a single vote. In general, then, the deal struck in the committee attracted enough supporters to ensure floor passage with only minor amendments.[98]

The House passed a mixed bag of changes. On one hand, it reversed several of the Senate's compromises by eliminating the cap on schools, requiring schools to be funded at 100 percent of a district's per-pupil operating revenue (PPOR), and reinstating the automatic waiver from state school law.[99] On the other, the House imposed a requirement that the state board of education hold its appeal hearings and make its decision in the district in which the proposed school would be located.[100] In the final moments, a slim bipartisan majority formed to pass the bill. With 63 representatives voting, 32 had to vote yes. As it turned out, there were not quite enough Republican yes votes to pass the bill, but at least five Democrats voted for the measure, putting it over the top.[101]

The conference committee moved the bill back in the direction of the Senate version by reinstating a cap (50 schools), case-by-case waivers, and funding negotiated with the local district (with a minimum of 80 percent of PPOR).[102] The conference also eliminated the requirement to hold appeal hearings in districts. But the conference committee added a couple of new wrinkles as well. First, it opened up the appeals process to individuals who wished to protest an *approval* of a charter. Second, it stipulated that on a first appeal the state board could only remand the decision for reconsideration. Only on the second appeal could it overturn a local board's action.[103]

Summary of Outcomes

As had happened in Massachusetts, the charter program in Colorado emerged with a mix of weaker and stronger provisions. On the weaker side, the law required charter applicants to approach their local school boards first. It also made charter schools legally part of their local school district, rather than independent schools. And instead of receiving automatic exemptions from state school law, charter schools had to ask local school boards and the state board of education for waivers on a case-by-case basis. On the stronger side, the law provided a narrow avenue for charter applicants rejected at the local level to appeal to the state board of education.

The Case of Georgia

Georgia's political terrain did not look like fertile ground for charter schools in 1993. Like most southern states a classic example of Elazar's traditionalistic political culture, Georgia lagged in both measures of economic advancement: its median income ($27,561) was below the national average, and relatively few (63.2 percent) of its citizens lived in cities.[104] In addition, Democrats occupied the governor's mansion and held wide majorities in the two houses of the legislature. More than any of the other states in this study, Georgia's charter school politics unfolded more or less as one would expect based on these general variables: a Democratic governor proposed a very weak charter bill, and the legislature weakened it further.

Context

The political context in Georgia in 1993 stood in striking contrast to that of the other three states in this study. First, no financial crisis loomed for Georgia's public schools. Quite to the contrary, Democratic governor Zell Miller had successfully asked voters to institute a lottery, which would soon generate hundreds of millions of dollars annually for K–12 education in Georgia. Further, with its rural population still large and politically strong, Georgia lacked the intense rural vs. nonrural conflict over finance present in the other states. The state did a reasonably good job of equalizing school spending, providing equalization funds amounting to 67.8 percent of average school spending in 1991–92.[105]

In Georgia, as in Colorado, education reform moments had come and gone, with the passage of the Quality Basic Education Act in 1985 and Miller's move to make local school boards elected and local superintendents appointed.[106] Though the Georgia Public Policy Foundation, a conservative think tank, had been lobbying vigorously for school vouchers, legislative support was so minimal that observers expected little discussion of the issue in the 1993 legislative session.[107]

In 1993, then, the education agenda in the legislature was virtually blank. The governor proposed to raise teachers' salaries by 5 percent and to raise the compulsory school age gradually from 16 to 18. Beyond those proposals, other than charter schools, the only item of the education agenda in the legislature was Georgia's perennial discussion of the nature of sex education in schools. Indeed, as the session got under way, the *Atlanta Journal and Constitution* wrote: "The legislature appears to be poised for inaction on education this session."[108]

Actors

As in other states in this study, the governor served as the catalyst for charter school legislation in Georgia. But Miller's motivation for introducing charter legislation was markedly different from Governor Engler's in Michigan and Governor Weld's in Massachusetts. Engler and Weld saw charter schools as a mechanism by which school reformers could bypass local school boards. Instead, like Colorado's Romer, Miller saw local school boards as the proper sites for school governance, according to Glenn Newsome, his education policy adviser.[109] The governor viewed charter schools as a way to induce *school districts* to innovate. Before 1993, a Georgia law had given local school districts the opportunity to ask the state board of education for waivers of state rules. But local districts had not come forward as Miller had hoped. The governor believed the possibility of converting schools to charter schools might prove more attractive. Miller's vision of charter schools, then, was not one of encouraging a broad range of "educational entrepreneurs" to come forward with new school designs. As his adviser paraphrased, Miller let it be known: "I am about improving public schools, not about creating new schools."

Whereas Engler, Weld, and even Romer had backed relatively strong charter bills, compromising later, Miller proposed a weaker program at the outset. The bill gave local boards the final say over the approval or denial of a charter application; placed charter schools under the legal authority of local boards; limited charter applicants to existing public schools, precluding startups; and required schools to approach the state board on a case-by-case basis to request waivers from state law and rules.[110] Arguably, with the requirement that only existing public schools could convert, and only then with the approval of the local school board, the bill was hardly a charter school proposal at all, but more of a school-based management initiative.

Miller enjoyed strong support in the legislature. Democrats outnumbered Republicans in the House 128 to 52 and in the Senate 41 to 15. To be sure, Republicans had gained strength in recent years. From 1965 to 1984, for example, the proportion of House seats held by Republicans hovered at around 13 percent. That figure had risen to nearly 30 percent by 1993.[111] Still, Democrats controlled affairs in Atlanta.

In the other states in this study, Republicans were more or less united in their support for charter school laws, and for stronger charter laws. In Georgia, however, the Republican Party split on the issue. On one side were legislators who, like their counterparts in other states, viewed charter schools as a way to inject some flexibility, choice, and competition into a public school system typified by rigidity and monopoly. On the other side were religious conservatives. To these Republicans, rigid and monopolistic public school districts were not necessarily problematic, as long as religious conservatives controlled local school boards. Since adherents to this political perspective had achieved wide success in Georgia's school districts, they feared that charter schools would bolster the efforts of liberal-minded educators to get out from under school board policies. Religious conservatives portrayed charter schools as a dangerous form of experimentation that would undermine "local control" of schools.[112]

In short, with the Democratic governor taking the initiative in proposing a very weak bill, the large Democratic majority backing him, and the small Republican minority not united behind charters, the legislative prospects for a strong charter bill in Georgia were bleak from the outset.

As in the other states, interest groups took notice of the charter proposal in Georgia. But because of the nature of Governor Miller's proposal, the pattern of interest group response differed markedly. Since local school boards had the final say over whether to approve charters, the school board association did not stand in the way of the charter bill. Those school boards that wanted the flexibility afforded by the law could pursue it; others could ignore it.[113] The superintendents' association was more wary, since local school boards could use the law to establish schools outside the superintendents' control. But on the whole, superintendents did not regard Miller's proposal as a significant threat.[114]

Georgia's NEA-affiliated teachers' association, the Georgia Association of Educators (GAE), was the education interest group most concerned about the proposed law. As noted above, Miller's proposal allowed only the conversion of an existing public school to charter status. The GAE took the position that a school should be allowed to convert only if a large majority of the school's faculty consented. Specifically, the GAE proposed three amendments: (1) that two-thirds of a school's faculty vote to approve a conversion to charter status; (2) that the vote be conducted by secret ballot; and (3) that the charter application include a proposal to involve the faculty "directly and substantially" in the converted school's planning and implementation.[115] With those changes, the GAE declared, it could support the proposal.

In general, analyses of interest group politics in Georgia have attributed little power to teacher and other educational groups. A recent study did remark that the GAE was "treated with a healthy respect because teachers in the legislators' home districts are numerous and likely to vote." The GAE was also the first state-level NEA affiliate to form a political action committee (PAC). But in this business-dominated state, the analysts concluded, teachers' influence was muted. The GAE's political action committee, for example, did not appear in the study's list of the 20 highest-contributing nonparty PACs.[116]

Process

The legislative debate centered on two points. First, in accordance with the wishes of the GAE, Senate Democrats pressed for provisions to strengthen the role of teachers in charter school affairs: requiring faculty involvement in crafting the charter plan, empowering the faculty of a charter school (with a two-thirds vote under secret ballot) to declare the charter null and void at any time, and requiring two-thirds of the faculty to sign off on any changes to the charter after initial approval.[117] With such wide Democratic majorities and the governor's backing, these proposals gained easy approval.

Second, conservative Republicans proposed numerous amendments to limit charter schools' ability to pursue radical paths of experimentation: amendments to require charter schools to follow the state's core curriculum, to eliminate references in the bill to "student outcomes" (which raised the specter of the feared "outcome-based education"), and to eliminate any role for the state board of education in charter school decisionmaking. Finally, they proposed amendments to ensure that parents in a school had a say over its conversion to charter status. Although most of the conservative amendments failed on the House and Senate floor, one succeeded: a provision requiring a two-thirds vote of parents to approve conversion to a charter.[118]

Summary of Outcomes

So in Georgia, an already weak initial proposal was further diluted in the legislative process. Governor Miller had proposed that local school boards have veto power over the creation of charter schools, but the legislature gave individual schools' teachers and parents veto power as well. In addition, schools received no automatic exemptions from school law; as in Colorado, they had to request them on a case-by-case basis from their local and state boards of education. The result was a bill that contained virtually all of the compromises one could imagine in a charter school law. The one exception: the law allowed an unlimited number of charter schools to form. With so many restrictions and veto points, however, this "strong" provision appeared unlikely to make much difference.

Discussion

These cases suggest four sources of variation in the outcomes of charter school politics. First is *the apparent importance of the broader legislative context in which charter schools were debated.* Among these four states, the two that passed the strongest charter laws, Massachusetts and Michigan, were the two in which the education policy agenda was packed with a host of pressing concerns other than charter schools. By contrast, in the two states with the weaker laws, Colorado and Georgia, the charter school bill stood out as one of the legislative session's most prominent education issues, if not the most prominent. The broader context appears to have made a difference in two different ways, usefully labeled "carrots" and "sticks." In Michigan and Massachusetts carrots seem to have increased the willingness of charter opponents to accept relatively strong bills. In both states, charter schools were debated alongside discussions of a complete overhaul of their systems of school finance. In both places, prospects looked bright for both a major increase in aggregate spending on schools and a major effort to equalize spending from district to district. Both of these changes appealed to education interest groups, but both seemed attainable only if accompanied by broader packages of quality reforms, including charter schools.

In Colorado and Georgia, no such carrots existed. Colorado had approved major school finance reform in 1988, and its voters had just voted down a proposal to increase the sales tax in order to pay for schools. Georgia's voters had recently approved a lottery that would increase school funding. But decisions about what to do with the additional money were not set to take place until after the 1993 legislative session, in which charters were debated. And finance inequities were not as severe as in Michigan and Massachusetts in any case. In neither Colorado nor Georgia, then, could proponents of strong charter legislation hold out the carrot of finance reform in exchange for acquiescence on charter schools.

Other items on the agenda played roles as sticks. In Michigan, the legislature took up proposals to study shutting down entire school districts, to sharply restrict the powers of teachers' unions, to abolish tenure, to impose statewide assessments with dire consequences for poorly performing districts, to institute a statewide system of interdistrict school choice, and other measures opposed by most education interest groups. Beyond that, a well-organized campaign to introduce school vouchers that could be spent at private and parochial schools was also under way. In Massachusetts, the legislature considered many of the same ideas. These proposed reforms had important consequences for the charter school debate. At the very least, they affected the amount of attention opponents of charter schools could devote to fighting the legislation; in both Michigan and Massachusetts, representatives of education interest groups made clear in interviews that they simply could not focus sufficient effort on charter schools in light of all of the other issues on the table. The presence of these reforms on the agenda may also have made charter schools look less threatening than they would have if, as in Georgia and

Colorado, charter schools stood virtually alone on the legislative docket. In comparison with losing tenure rights and the closed shop, for example, the prospect of a handful of charter schools may have seemed trivial to Michigan's teachers' unions.

The broader legislative agenda (or lack thereof) grew directly out of the economic factors found to be important in the previous chapter's quantitative analysis. In Massachusetts and Michigan, economic progress advanced unevenly, with rural school districts feeling the pinch as urban or suburban areas grew in population and prosperity. Since these states had done little by 1993 to address rural districts' fiscal problems, the stage was set for ferocious political battles in both states over school finance, out of which charter school programs arose. Colorado's economic picture was much the same, but its school finance battle had come and gone by the time charter schools emerged on the national political scene. Otherwise, charter school politics in Colorado might have more closely resembled that in Michigan and Massachusetts. Georgia, poorer and more rural than the other three states, was less subject to these conflicts. Strong in the legislature, rural districts had been more successful historically gaining resources for their schools; unlike their counterparts in Michigan and Massachusetts, they were not primed for a school finance fight in 1993.

Context alone, however, is not sufficient to account for differences in these four states. A second influence on the legislative variation was *gubernatorial leadership*. In Michigan and Massachusetts, the broader legislative agenda served as carrot and stick because Republican governors made strategic choices to use context for that purpose. Governor Engler set forth an explicit ultimatum: without substantial "quality reform," he would not agree to expand or reslice the pie of educational resources. This ultimatum created the carrot that brought opponents of reform, including charter schools, to the table. Engler also crafted an arsenal of sticks: the prospect of radical educational change, including a charter bill that would have created literally hundreds of potential chartering authorities. Governor Weld in Massachusetts pursued much the same strategy. By making such bold proposals, Engler and Weld effectively shifted the political center of gravity in a direction of more major change.

In Georgia, Democratic governor Miller followed a much different approach. Viewing charters as a way to give local school boards the chance to innovate, he proposed a very limited charter bill at the outset. There was not much compromising to do from that starting point. If Engler and Weld shifted the center of gravity in the direction of major change, Governor Miller did the opposite, setting in motion a process likely to result in a very weak charter law. Gubernatorial leadership was thus important in Georgia as well, but with dramatically different consequences.

Colorado's story is somewhat different, but the governor still loomed large. Democrat Romer did not initiate charter legislation as his counterparts did in the other three states. Instead he set forth some parameters under which he would accept charter legislation. The critical parameter was that the law leave substantial authority in the hands of local school boards. Knowing they could not win approval without the governor's backing, legislators crafted a compromise bill that granted local boards a major role in the approval and oversight of charter schools. With this concession, Romer became a significant advocate for charter schools, playing a major role in guiding the modified bill through the legislature.

A third influence on the legislative outcome was *partisan control of the legislature.* These four states exhibited four different partisan configurations: in Colorado, Republicans controlled both houses and there was a Democratic governor; in Michigan, Republicans controlled the Senate, the House was evenly split, and there was a Republican governor; and in Massachusetts and Georgia, Democrats controlled both houses, but Massachusetts had a Republican governor and Georgia a Democratic one. The outcomes in Michigan, Georgia, and Colorado approximated what one might have expected given their partisan configurations.

In Michigan, Republicans were well positioned to press for a strong charter law, especially with their compatriot in the governor's office. If legislative Republicans remained united, they needed to persuade only one Democrat in the House to support them in order to secure passage of any measure. In Georgia, by contrast, Democrats controlled both houses of the legislature as well as the governor's office. Even if the Republican Party had united behind strong charter legislation, it would not have had a chance to see it enacted. As it turns out, religious and free-market conservatives could not agree, making a strong charter law even more of a pipe dream there. Colorado passed a charter law of mid-dling strength despite its two Republican houses of the legislature. Hav-ing narrowed the Republican margin in both houses in the 1992 elections, Democrats had the numbers to uphold a gubernatorial veto. Thus, al-though they controlled neither house, Democrats were in a position to exact compromises, and they did so.

Massachusetts confounds these straightforward partisan stories, but only slightly. With two Democratic houses and a Republican governor, one might have expected a bill containing more compromises than the relatively strong law Massachusetts enacted. But from the beginning of the education reform debate in 1991, legislative Democrats had backed a relatively strong form of charter legislation. Two factors appear to have accounted for the Democrats' willingness to resist the traditional pres-sures of Democratic interest group politics. First, the stakes of the over-all education reform debate were very high. Democratic leaders made a judgment that to obtain higher and more equitable funding for schools they would have to offer up quality reforms. Ultimately, they gambled, Democratic constituents would be so pleased with the financial bonanza that they would forgive the legislators' willingness to break ranks on re-form issues. Second, and perhaps more important, many Democratic leaders backed charter legislation that was strong in many respects *but that capped the number of charter schools at a very low number.* Agree-ment on the cap, in effect, made the stronger components of the law (like the significant autonomy granted to charter schools) "safe" in the eyes of Democrats. How much harm could charter schools—even highly autonomous ones—do to traditional Democratic constituencies if there were only 25 of them?

A final observation concerns *the role of the teachers' associations.* Al-though teachers' groups in all four states opposed strong charter legisla-tion, their varied success bears no apparent relationship to their political strength. Michigan's MEA, regarded as one of the most potent political forces in that state, saw one of the nation's strongest charter laws en-acted. Georgia's GAE, not thought of as a major player in state politics, saw one of the nation's weakest laws introduced and was able to weaken it even further in the legislature.

Teachers' power seems to have been almost entirely contingent on the other variables discussed here—political context, gubernatorial leadership, and partisan configuration. Michigan provides the best illustration. The MEA's legendary power relied almost entirely on its influence over the Democratic Party. Though historically speaking that channel had served the MEA well, it did no good in 1993, when Democrats wielded little authority. Even if almost all Democrats had been under the MEA's thumb, the MEA would have had trouble stopping Republicans from enacting a legislative program. The MEA further suffered because of the political context: the broader legislative agenda in which charter schools were embedded. As much as the MEA would liked to have stopped charter schools, much higher priorities were winning finance reform and avoiding some of Governor Engler's more draconian proposals to limit union power directly. In the midst of all of this, Engler successfully made the MEA's strength a liability, blunting the union's ability to make its case to the public. Against this backdrop, the MEA's ability to mobilize voters and money was of little consequence. The observation in Chapter 2 that strong laws were likely to emerge in states with both Republican strength *and* union strength is illustrated nicely by what happened in Michigan, where the collision of these two forces helped propel the charter law (and other reforms) forward.

In Massachusetts and Colorado, teachers' unions were also undermined by the willingness of Democratic political leaders to back relatively strong charter school provisions. Like the MEA, teachers' groups in these two states had to look to Democrats for influence. But Democratic legislators in Massachusetts supported highly independent charter schools; the Democratic governor of Colorado put his support behind a provision allowing charter applicants rejected by their local school boards to appeal to the state board of education. As in Michigan, the power of teachers' associations depended heavily on factors beyond their electoral or financial strength.

Conclusion

In all four states, charter school proponents found that they had to compromise on important issues in order to win passage of charter school legislation. They had to choose between an impure form of charter schools and no charter schools at all. To be sure, the magnitude of the compromises varied from state to state. But compromise has pervaded the politics of charter schools everywhere they have been proposed.[119]

Debates over charter schools took months and even years to resolve, but eventually all four of the state legislatures enacted charter school laws. However, the road to charter schools did not end with the adoption of legislation. In each state, attention turned to implementation, to putting into place what legislators had crafted in the heat of politics.

Charter School Programs in Practice

II

4 | *Breaking the Mold*

H AVE POLITICAL compromises hampered the effective implementation of charter school programs? To set the stage for that discussion, I first set forth a framework for evaluating the potential of charter school programs to fulfill their promise.

Off the Drawing Board

The first charter school opened in Minnesota in 1992; most charter schools are less than two years old. Since building a school from scratch takes time, it is too early to say whether charter schools, on average, are successful as schools. So-called second-order effects—the hoped-for influence charter schools will have on regular public schools—are likely to be even longer in the making, though some evidence on district responses has begun to emerge.[1] One might argue that it is simply too early to tell whether charter school programs are successful.

On the contrary, I believe that we have enough experience with charter school programs to evaluate their *potential* to achieve the results their proponents envision. In particular, four conditions must be met for the hopes of charter school proponents to be realized: autonomy, viability, impact, and accountability.

1. Autonomy: *Charter schools must enjoy sufficient autonomy to differentiate themselves from conventional public schools.* Without the freedom to be different in some significant ways, charter schools cannot fulfill any of their intended purposes. They cannot provide unique educational options for children. They cannot serve as experimental models for public schools. And they cannot compete with conventional public school systems for students in any meaningful fashion.

2. Viability: *Charter schools that succeed in attracting students and meet their legal and contractual obligations must be potentially viable as organizations.* Certainly, not all charter schools will succeed in attracting students or in living up to their obligations under their charters or under the law. It is not, therefore, a condition of success that *all* charter schools be viable as organizations. But an effective charter school program must be one in which successful charter schools can survive financially. If the program is set up so that even a charter school with a squeaky-clean record, top-notch academic results, and hundreds of children on its waiting list cannot make ends meet, it will fail.

3. Impact: *The charter school "sector" must have the potential, through competition or by example, to have a significant positive impact on regular public schools.* The first two conditions are necessary underpinnings of the third: if charter schools are not granted autonomy or are not able to survive as organizations, their potential for impact is minimal. But these two conditions are not sufficient. The programs must also be designed so that these autonomous, viable charter schools exert some influence over regular schools, through competition or by example, or improve public education through some other channel. To be sure, if charter schools provide superior educational options for some children, one might regard them as successful. But to achieve the *full* potential envisioned by charter school advocates, charter schools need to have an influence on other schools and on students other than their own.

4. Accountability: *Charter schools must be held accountable for academic results, not only by families as "customers" but also by a public authority.* A

unique feature of charter schools as a form of school choice is that, in order to retain their charters, participating schools must meet ambitious targets for student performance. For charter school programs to succeed, public authorities responsible for charter schools must institute systems of accountability that genuinely hold charter schools to this test.

This and the following two chapters take up the first three conditions for successful charter school programs. In general, legislative compromises, especially in Georgia, have had a significant impact on how well charter school programs function. But the experience of the four states also suggests that what happened in their state legislatures in 1993 did not fully determine the course of their charter programs. Postadoption politics, strategies pursued by implementers, and unexpected consequences also had a major effect on how charter school programs turned out.

I do not devote an entire chapter to the fourth condition, accountability, because legislative compromises on issues of accountability for charter schools have been minimal. Most state legislatures have passed relatively standard, largely vague provisions stating that charter schools are to be held accountable for results. In this study of the effects of legislative compromise on the functioning of charter school programs, then, there is little to say about accountability. But since accountability is so essential to the charter idea, Chapter 7 devotes some attention to how charter school programs have handled issues of accountability.

To explore the consequences of legislative compromise, I return to the four states examined in the previous chapter: Colorado, Georgia, Massachusetts, and Michigan. Having passed such different charter school laws, they provide an opportunity to analyze how different patterns of compromise have played out in practice. Here I trace the implementation of the charter school legislation adopted in 1993 through the end of the 1995–96 school year. By that time, charter schools in all four states had been operating for at least one year; some schools in Michigan and Colorado had been open for two years.

Interviews, public documents, and news reports informed my analysis of charter school implementation. In each state I interviewed (1) the state government official or officials responsible for implementation of the charter school program; (2) representatives of public bodies responsible for approving and overseeing charter schools, if different from the state officials; (3) representatives of at least three charter schools (two in Georgia, which had only three schools); (4) representatives of organizations dedicated to supporting the development of charter schools; (5) political leaders and staff involved in crafting and monitoring charter legislation (governors' aides, legislators, and legislative staff). Altogether, I interviewed 51 individuals for this study.

Because the process of charter school selection and oversight differs from state to state, the types of public documents differ from state to state as well. In general, though, public documents included: charter school regulations; materials documenting the charter school selection process, such as application materials and scoring rubrics; charter school applications; records of proceedings of bodies charged with reviewing charter school applications; official documents produced in the review of charter school applications; profiles of approved charter schools; actual "charters," or contracts between charter schools and their authorizing agencies; official correspondence sent by authorizing agencies to all charter schools explaining policies and procedures; reports by authorizing agencies on the progress of the charter school program; reports by outside agencies on the progress of the charter school program; and annual reports prepared by charter schools on their finances and operations. In addition, I reviewed more than 400 news stories on the progress of charter school programs.

Autonomy in Charter School Programs

Perhaps no concept is as central to the charter school idea as "autonomy." Without autonomy, charter schools cannot provide unique educational options for children. They cannot serve as experimental "laboratories" or "lighthouses" from which other schools can learn. And they cannot act as market competitors, threatening the public school monopoly and inducing it to change. Autonomy enables one of the three conditions of success for charter school programs: differentiation. The autonomy of charter schools is clearly one potential target for legislative opponents of charter school programs. This chapter looks at how legislative compromises have affected charter schools' autonomy, their potential to differentiate themselves educationally and otherwise from prevailing practices.

The evidence from the four states presents an interesting picture. One state, Georgia, passed a law so restrictive that charter schools had virtually no more autonomy than conventional public schools. But while the charter laws in the other three states, Colorado, Massachusetts, and Michigan, contained autonomy-threatening provisions, charter schools in all three reported wide latitude in the conduct of their affairs. Two factors appear to have influenced this paradoxical pattern. First, political circumstances in these three states *after* the laws passed favored autonomy and differentiation. So although the laws themselves looked restrictive in some ways, postadoption politics made them permissive. Second, although charter schools were subject to many unexpected laws and regulations, these tended not to constrain them on the core elements of running their schools. Though highly regulated in many ways, charter schools were free to make the most important decisions for themselves.

Two factors are particularly important in determining how autonomous charter schools are in a state. The most obvious is the degree of freedom charter schools experience once they are open and operating. For example, how much control do charter schools have over the hiring of teachers? The allocation of funds? The selection of curriculum and instructional methods? Differentiation in charter school programs is also affected by the criteria used to approve charter schools. Charter school laws place the authority to approve or deny charter schools in the hands of one or more public bodies. The legislation may spell out some general criteria these bodies must use, but charter laws generally allow the decisionmakers a great deal of discretion. If the decisionmakers approve only those applications that meet narrow criteria, they undermine differentiation. This chapter explores these two factors affecting charter school autonomy in Colorado, Georgia, Massachusetts, and Michigan.

Selecting Charter Schools

The four states in this study adopted charter school laws that called for very different selection processes. Two differences set the states apart: the range of public bodies empowered to authorize charter schools, and the range of individuals and organizations allowed to organize charter schools. At one extreme was Michigan's law, which empowered a relatively wide range of public bodies to charter schools, including the boards of local school districts, intermediate school districts, community colleges, and public universities.[2] At the other extreme was Georgia's law, which invested only local school boards with the power to charter schools (and only then with the approval of the state board of education). The Massachusetts law placed the authority in the hands of a single gubernatorial appointee: the secretary of education.[3] Colorado required charter organizers to approach their local boards for approval first, but local boards' decisions could be appealed to the state board of education, which had the power to overturn local decisions.

On the question of who could apply for charter status, the four laws also differed. Again, Michigan's was the most open, allowing any individual or organization except religious organizations (such as parochial schools) to apply. Massachusetts imposed this same restriction, but also excluded nonreligious private schools from seeking charter status. Colorado's law did the same; it also prohibited home-based schools from becoming charter schools. Georgia's law was, again, the most restrictive, allowing only existing public schools to convert to charter status. No outside groups or individuals could apply for a charter in Georgia.[4]

Of these four laws, one would expect Michigan's selection process to yield the greatest differentiation. With such a large number of possible authorizers, even if particular authorizers had strong preferences about the types of schools they would charter, charter organizers could shop around for an authorizer with a compatible orientation. And since the range of potential organizers was relatively wide, one would expect a variety of prospective charter schools to be doing this shopping. Georgia's law, by contrast, would be expected to yield the lowest differentiation. Chartering authority rested with those entities that already had the power to determine the range of educational options in the community. And before the charter law, Georgia already had legislation allowing districts to seek waivers from state policy. In a sense, then, Georgia's charter law did not substantially change the regulatory framework governing school districts. Combined with the fact that only existing schools (with existing staffs, student bodies, and so on) could apply for charter status, this minimal change in the legal framework did not appear likely to change the status quo.

Colorado and Massachusetts fell somewhere in between. Though the Colorado law provided a nonlocal alternative, it placed some high hurdles—in particular a cumbersome appeals process—in the way of charter applicants' ability to take advantage of it. The Massachusetts law gave no authority to local school boards but vested all power in the hands of one person. Unlike Michigan, then, neither Massachusetts nor Colorado allowed charter applicants to shop around for potential authorizers. If the single state authority said no, the petitioners were out of luck. One might expect these provisions to place Colorado and Massachusetts somewhere between Michigan and Georgia on the continuum.

To explore how these expectations have been borne out in practice, this section considers two measures of state programs' differentiation: the speed of proliferation of charter schools in each state, and the breadth of design approaches approved in each state.

Proliferation

By the 1995–96 school year, Michigan had the most charter schools in operation, Georgia the least, Colorado and Massachusetts somewhere in between (see Figure 4-1). Given the number of charter schools in each state, one might conclude that a program's differentiation is related to the extent of legislative compromise on the issues of who can apply and who can approve. Taking account of population differences between the states, however, makes the picture more complex. Colorado has the most charter schools per capita, with one school for every 156,000 residents in 1995. Otherwise, the states stay in the same order: Michigan has one for every 233,000 residents, Massachusetts one for every 405,000 residents, and Georgia one for every 2.4 million residents.[5]

A closer look suggests that postadoption state politics played a critical role in determining differentiation in at least three of these four states. The placement of authority in nonlocal hands appears to have been a necessary, but not sufficient, condition for significant proliferation of charter schools.

Figure 4-1. *Number of Charter Schools in Operation in Michigan, Colorado, Massachusetts, and Georgia, 1995–96*

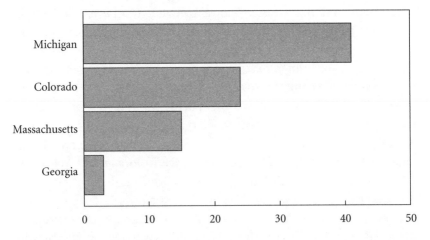

Sources: Colorado Department of Education, "Colorado Charter Schools: Charter Schools Approved and Operating," November 15, 1995; Massachusetts Department of Education, *The Massachusetts Charter School Initiative: 1996 Report* (Boston, 1996); Michigan Department of Education, *A Description of Michigan Public School Academies: 1995–96 Report to the House and Senate Committees in Education* (Lansing, 1996); Georgia Department of Education, "Georgia Charter School Program. Annual Report Summaries: School Year 1996–97" [sic—actually 1995–96], ca.1996.

Colorado. By the beginning of the 1995–96 school year, the Colorado state board had held hearings on appeals from 25 different charter school applicants. Of these 25, the board remanded applications to local boards or overturned local decisions in eight cases and upheld the local board decisions on the other 17 schools. Of the 24 schools open in the fall of 1995, four had initially been rejected and had received charters only after the state board remanded their applications to local boards for reconsideration.[6]

In light of these facts, how important was the appeal provision of Colorado's charter law? On the one hand, 20 of 24 charter schools received approval locally without having to file appeals with the state. Further, the state upheld local decisions most of the time. On the other hand, the state board of education proved itself willing to remand or even overturn local decisions, doing so as early as April 1994. While impossible to quantify, this willingness arguably induced some local boards to approve applications they might otherwise have rejected.

But the mere existence of a statutory provision empowering the state board of education to override local boards only made these actions *possible*. For the provision to have any teeth, the state board had to be willing to act on its authority. And since state board members are elected by the public, this willingness was inherently contingent on politics. If the public had elected a board of education majority that believed in deferring to local authority on the chartering of schools, the outcome in Colorado would probably have been much different. So while the legislation authorizing appeals may have contributed to the proliferation of charter schools in Colorado, it was not a sufficient condition.

Massachusetts. In the first application cycle, 100 groups submitted proposals to the secretary of education. The secretary granted charters to 21, and 15 of the schools managed to open for the 1995–96 school year. Because there was no local involvement in the process, it is impossible to know how many of these schools would have been approved by local school committees. Many of the chartered schools, however, reported encountering hostility to their existence from local school officials, implying that they would not have faced smooth sailing at the local level.[7]

The placement of authority in state hands, then, appears to have opened up the possibility for a significant amount of chartering. As in Colorado, though, the legislative language was necessary but not sufficient. From the passage of the law through the period covered by this study, the secretary of education was appointed by Republican governor William Weld, who, as described in Chapter 3, favored an expansive charter school program with a high degree of differentiation. With a friend of charter schools as governor, chartering proceeded apace. Had a person with a different outlook held the position, the outcome could well have differed greatly.

Michigan. Michigan's law was most remarkable for the sheer number of potential chartering agencies. Michigan has 521 local school districts, 51 intermediate school districts, 28 community colleges, and 15 public universities; the board of any of these agencies has the power to charter

Table 4-1. *Michigan Educational Bodies That Authorized Charter Schools to Open in 1995–96*

Characteristics	Local school boards (N = 521)	Intermediate school boards (N = 51)	Community college boards (N = 28)	University boards (N = 15)
Number that had chartered schools	2	6	0	3
Percentage that had chartered schools	0.4	11.8	0	20.0
Number of schools chartered	3	7	0	31
Percentage of all Michigan schools chartered	7.3	17.1	0	75.6

Source: Michigan Department of Education, *A Description of Michigan Public School Academies: 1995–96 Report to the House and Senate Committees in Education* (Lansing, 1996).

a. Data refer only to schools open during the 1995–96 school year.

schools. But chartering activity has not been spread evenly among these entities (see Table 4-1).

Through the 1995–96 school year, only two of the state's 521 school districts had chartered schools that were up and running (the Detroit and Wyoming districts); only six of the state's 51 intermediate school districts had done so. No operating charter school had been chartered by a community college. By contrast, more than three-quarters (31 of 41) operating charter schools had been chartered by university boards of trustees; and more than four-fifths of those (26 of 31) were chartered by a single institution: Central Michigan University (CMU) in Mount Pleasant.[8]

The dominance of a university in the chartering business was not a foregone conclusion in Michigan. Within a month of the law's passage, university officials were casting public doubt on whether universities would play a major role in the charter program. Education schools, the most natural sites for charter-related activity, tended to have close ties with existing school districts, which they relied upon for student teacher placements and access for research purposes. The prospect of authorizing schools to compete with these longtime partners was unattractive to many university personnel. As the dean of the Grand Valley State University school of education put it: "We're certainly not going to risk our relationship with them [local school districts] just for the chance to create our own school." Universities also worried about the cost of reviewing charter applications, providing help to applicants and schools, and monitoring the schools.[9] Ultimately, Central Michigan was the only university to enter the charter arena aggressively. Only two other universities had chartered schools that were open in the 1995–96 school year, and they initially limited their chartering to their own geographic areas. By contrast, CMU announced its intention to charter schools all over the state of Michigan.

So Michigan's experience accords with the pattern in the other two states. By casting a wide net, the law made it *possible* for CMU to emerge as the state's de facto statewide chartering authority. As in the other states, politics proved critical: the trustees of public universities are appointed by the governor. As the chapter on the politics of charter schools in Michigan noted, Governor Engler was a major proponent of charter schools in the legislature. Once the bill passed, Engler turned his attention in part to persuading university boards to participate actively in the chartering process. He received an especially open hearing at his alma mater, CMU, whose board was chaired by W. Sydney Smith, characterized in the press as the governor's "longtime friend." In subsequent legislative sessions, Engler lobbied for special funding to seed a resource center for charter schools at CMU.[10]

The proliferation of charter schools in Michigan, then, was contingent on postadoption politics. The mere existence of multiple chartering authorities did not guarantee a vibrant charter movement. Indeed, had CMU not moved aggressively, Michigan's charter program might well have grown anemically by national standards.[11]

Georgia. The circumstances in Georgia were much more straightforward. In granting sole chartering authority to local school boards, the charter law left no scope for postadoption state politics to influence the outcome. After the legislation passed, the state department of education held some 400 information sessions around the state to promote interest in charter schools. Though many schools expressed initial enthusiasm, almost all potential applicants decided not to move forward. Some tested the waters with their local school boards and found the charter idea unwelcome. Others went to the public and encountered opposition from religious conservative organizations opposed to what they viewed as "radical experimentation" in education. In the end, only three charter applicants even approached their local school boards formally before the 1995–96 school year. All three were approved and began operating as charter schools. But countless others decided not to move forward because they anticipated opposition.[12]

With the exception of Georgia, then, the impact of the selection process on the proliferation of charter schools followed a similar pattern in these states. The charter legislation in each of the three states made it possible for state-level entities to encourage the proliferation of charter schools, but they did not mandate it. Only because state politics were tilted in favor of differentiation did proliferation occur.

Departures from Conventional Practice

Differentiation refers not only to how many charter schools emerge but also to whether they are allowed to depart from conventional ways of doing things. A charter program that authorized dozens of charter schools, but only those that fit into a conventional mold, would not exhibit much differentiation.

One would expect that in states like Georgia and Colorado, where local boards played a large role in chartering, charter schools would depart less from conventional practice than in states like Michigan and Massachusetts, where charter applicants had alternative routes of authorization. The experience in Georgia certainly conformed to this expectation. Not only did few charter schools emerge there; those that emerged departed only minimally from existing practice. In Colorado, by contrast, the degree of departure looked similar to that in Michigan and Massachusetts.

In Georgia, only three charter schools opened for business in the 1995–96 school year. As required by Georgia's law, all were conversions of existing public schools. And these schools departed only minimally from their precharter practice. One school requested exemption in just one area: a waiver of requirements for curriculum-based assessment in grades

Table 4-2. *Enrollment in Charter Schools, by State, 1995–96*

Enrollment	Colorado	Massachusetts	Michigan
	Percentage distribution		
50 or fewer	13	7	27
51–100	26	26	19
101–200	35	47	39
201–400	22	7	15
401 or more	4	13	0
	Number		
Average for charter schools	153	171	124
Average for charter high schools	120	75	93
Average for public schools	440	490	477

Sources: Colorado Department of Education, "Colorado Charter Schools: Charter Schools Approved and Operating," November 15, 1995; Massachusetts Department of Education, *The Massachusetts Charter School Initiative: 1996 Report* (Boston, 1996); Michigan Department of Education, *Description of Michigan Public School Academies.* Overall public school averages from National Center for Education Statistics, *Digest of Educational Statistics* (U.S. Department of Education, 1995), tables 39, 95.

three and five. A second school, already a unique magnet school (the only public Montessori academy in Georgia), asked only to add sixth graders to its K–5 enrollment and to give "priority acceptance" to minority prekindergarten students living in its attendance zone. A third school requested few legal exemptions and appears to have used the charter law primarily to enhance the role of its community/parent/staff advisory board.[13] In short, Georgia's charter schools departed only slightly from their precharter practices.

In Colorado, Michigan, and Massachusetts, however, a wide range of schools were chartered in 1995–96. This diversity is evident on three measures: school size, curricular focus, and target population.

Charter schools in all three states had a wide range of school enrollments (see Table 4-2). Michigan had a higher proportion of very small schools, Massachusetts a higher fraction of very large ones. In all three, though, average enrollment was much lower than the average enrollment in public schools in these states. Charter high schools are even smaller, on average, than charter schools in general; in Massachusetts

Table 4-3. *Curricular Approach of Charter Schools in Colorado,*
Massachusetts, and Michigan, 1995–96

Percent

Approach	Colorado	Massachusetts	Michigan[a]
General/not identifiable	13	33	24
Basics	21	12	15
Culture-centric	0	7	15
Subject focus (for example, arts or science/math)	4	0	10
Vocational	4	7	15
Alternative (for example, Montessori, Paideia)	58	40	22

Sources: Colorado Department of Education, "Colorado Charter Schools"; Massachusetts Department of Education, *Massachusetts Charter School Initiative;* Michigan Department of Education, *Description of Michigan Public School Academies.*

a. Michigan's percentages do not add to 100 because of rounding.

and Michigan charter high school had an average enrollment of fewer than 100 students.[14]

Charter schools in these states also took diverse curricular approaches. Table 4-3 categorizes the schools according to the predominant theme of the official descriptions found in state documents, though it does not do justice to the nuances that differentiate the 80 schools profiled. The "Alternative" category, which accounts for the largest percentage of schools, itself contains quite a number of different kinds of schools. Michigan's schools were the most diverse on this measure, with 10 percent or more schools in all six categories. Massachusetts's and Colorado's schools were more concentrated in the General, Basics, and Alternative categories.

A majority of schools in all three states targeted a general population of students, but a substantial number in Massachusetts and Michigan targeted a more specific segment (see Table 4-4). In Michigan, more than four in ten charter schools focused on a specific ethnic minority, at-risk students, or special-needs children. Colorado's schools, by contrast, served an overwhelmingly "general" student population.

In all three states, then, the selection process admitted a wide range of charter schools. Applicants were not channeled into a narrow concep-

Table 4-4. *Target Populations of Charter Schools in Colorado,*
Massachusetts, and Michigan, 1995–96

Percent

Target population	Colorado	Massachusetts	Michigan[a]
General	88	67	59
Ethnic minority	0	13	22
At risk	8	20	15
Special needs	0	0	5
Gifted	4	0	0

Sources: Colorado Department of Education, "Colorado Charter Schools"; Massachusetts Department of Education, *Massachusetts Charter School Initiative;* Michigan Department of Education, *Description of Michigan Public School Academies.*

a. Michigan's percentages do not add to 100 because of rounding.

tion of what kinds of students to focus on, what educational approach to take, or how large to be. And with the exception of target population, charter schools in Colorado were just as varied as those in Massachusetts and Michigan.

These patterns may be explained by the selection processes used in the three states. In Massachusetts, though a single official made all charter decisions in this time period, the selection criteria did not skew decisionmaking toward particular approaches, sizes, or target populations. For example, on instructional approach, the scoring rubric gave high marks to applicants that exhibited "innovative teaching method and curricular approaches"; a "commitment to high academic standards for all students"; "clear, measurable goals around which to build the educational program"; and "consistency between mission and the educational programs"—none of which suggested that applicants ought to follow one school of thought over another with regard to curriculum or pedagogy. On target population, the process rewarded applicants who displayed "an understanding of, and sensitivity for, the students to be served," but it did not tilt the scales toward any particular group of students. Instead, the application emphasized the "strength and commitment of the founding/management team," the viability of the proposed school as a business, and the steps the founders envisioned to implement their ideas. The focus rested squarely on the applicants' capacity to carry out what they proposed, rather than on whether what they proposed fit some predetermined model.[15]

Central Michigan University, which has chartered most of Michigan's charter schools, similarly stressed the capability of the applicants, not any particular idea of what the schools should be like. As in Massachusetts, the application materials asked applicants to explain their educational goals, methods of assessment, curriculum and pedagogy, and target population, and the scoring rubric did not reward applicants who follow one approach or another.[16]

Political circumstances made it possible for reviewers in both the Massachusetts Executive Office of Education and the Central Michigan University Charter Schools Office to apply such broadminded criteria. The result was a wide differentiation of schools in both states. In Colorado, by contrast, one might have expected the heavy involvement of local school boards to channel applicants into narrow curricular or pedagogical gaps. The data suggest that this did not happen. One possibility, discussed above, is that the potency of the state board of education's appeal process made it untenable for local school boards to reject applicants whose instructional approaches they did not like. But analysis of decisionmaking in the Denver public school system presents another possibility: that while local school boards often resisted the opening of charter schools, they rarely did so because they opposed the instructional approaches the charter applicants put forward.

Sixteen applicants approached the school board of Denver Public Schools (DPS) before the 1995–96 school year. Only two schools were approved and open for business in 1995–96. Most were turned down outright; others were approved with conditions that prevented their opening by that time. The two schools that received approval and opened were Clayton Charter School and P.S. 1. Of the many rejected applications, the one from Thurgood Marshall Charter Middle School received the most attention.

Of the three, Clayton encountered the smoothest sailing. The applicant, the Clayton Foundation, was a pre-existing organization that worked with at-risk young people in a section of Denver. Clayton proposed to extend its popular and successful child-care program into the elementary years. DPS said yes without much objection. But three important factors worked in Clayton's favor. First, the proposed school was small, initially planning to educate only 88 students out of DPS's enrollment of more than 60,000. Second, Clayton brought substantial financial resources to the table. It would draw down some per-pupil funds from the district, but it also pledged to provide $1.42 million of its own funds over three years. The school system, by contrast, would only have to spend $110,814 on Clayton in the first year, according to a DPS analysis. In effect, Clayton offered to educate some of the system's most difficult-to-educate students, matching public dollars many times over with private resources.[17] Third, Clayton owned a facility that would house the school. DPS would not have to provide space or offer funding for the renovation of a building.[18]

Together, these factors meant that the fiscal impact of Clayton Charter School on DPS would be minuscule. And fiscal impact was at the forefront of DPS officials' minds in early 1994. As the board vetted charter proposals, DPS announced a $15 million budget deficit for the 1994–95 school year. At the same time, the board was considering two expensive initiatives: a $4 million effort to front-load resources on the early grades, and a $6 million 3.5 percent pay increase for the system's teachers. In this climate, only a charter school proposal with a minimal budgetary impact looked attractive.[19]

The proposal for P.S. 1 was spearheaded by Rex Brown, a well-connected public policy analyst at the Denver-based Education Commission of the States who had advocated for charter legislation. In February 1994 the board rejected P.S. 1's application.[20] A primary consideration was the school's proposed enrollment of 200, which would cost DPS $601,609 in the first year, nearly six times Clayton's price tag. The following year, DPS approved P.S. 1's application, but only on the condition that P.S. 1 raise its *entire budget* from non-DPS sources. In response, P.S. 1 undertook a massive lobbying campaign, invoking the support of the governor, the mayor, business leaders, neighborhood activists, and city council members.[21] P.S. 1 also filed an appeal with the state board, which voted 6 to 1 in May to remand the application to the local board for reconsideration.[22] In the end, on a 4 to 3 vote in June, the Denver board reversed itself. But the price was a reduction of the number of students to a mere 60, and a cap on funding at 90 percent of DPS's per-pupil operating revenue, less than $4,000 per student. This arrangement yielded a total first-year cost to the district of about $120,000, roughly comparable to Clayton's price tag.[23]

Notably, district officials praised P.S. 1's design throughout the process. DPS had actually invited Brown to submit an application. The 14-member panel DPS set up in 1994 to review charter applications concluded that P.S. 1's concept has "potential, seeks to fill a void in the urban center, and is unique and innovative."[24] Upon reconsideration, a similar 1995 panel voted unanimously to support P.S. 1's application. On the eve of the first 1995 vote, school board president Tom Mauro told the press: "I think if we had the money, P.S. 1 would be a slam dunk. But we don't have the money."[25]

A third proposal came from a team led by Cordia Booth, a middle-school teacher in the Denver Public Schools, for the Thurgood Marshall Charter Middle School (TMCMS). Like P.S. 1, TMCMS proposed a relatively large enrollment—216 in the first year and larger after that. DPS calculated an initial-year cost of $861,983, nearly eight times the size of Clayton's.[26] Further, TMCMS organizers asked for even more money than that. Colorado's charter law requires districts and charter schools to negotiate the particulars of their per-pupil funding, but to begin the discussions at 80 percent of the district's "per-pupil operating revenue," or PPOR. PPOR is a very specific measure that excludes quite a few sources of school revenue. Accordingly, TMCMS asked for its funding to be based instead on a broader measure of average operating revenues: *total* general fund revenues divided by the number of students. In addition, TMCMS asked for 93 percent of this amount, not 80 percent, for a total of almost $2 million in the first year. Finally, TMCMS requested the use of a district facility and a host of services including payroll, accounting, special education, and maintenance.[27]

In February 1994 the board rejected TMCMS's application, sparking what became the most protracted charter school–related dispute in Colorado.[28] On April 6, 1994, the state board of education remanded the decision to the local board for reconsideration.[29] In May, the Denver board again said no.[30] The state board, however, overrode the local board again in July, ordering DPS to allow TMCMS to open in the 1995–96 school year.[31] Through the fall of 1995, DPS and TMCMS officials worked to come to some agreement over the opening and functioning of the school.

But in February 1995, TMCMS filed suit in District Court, alleging that DPS was not following the state board's mandate to have TMCMS open by the fall of 1995. In March the District Court enjoined DPS to abide by the state board's ruling. But in June the judge stayed his injunction, further delaying the school's opening.[32]

Because of all of the school district analysis, school board debates, and, ultimately, court filings, an extensive paper trail exists on the dispute over TMCMS. As in the case of P.S. 1, little of it related to the educational program TMCMS proposed to offer. When DPS officials and board members did discuss TMCMS's ideas about schooling, they almost always did so in laudatory terms.[33] The only issues explicitly mentioned as standing in the way of approval were the school's site and funding. As late as October 1995, in the middle of a court battle with TMCMS organizers, Denver school board president Aaron Gray remarked: "Thurgood Marshall cannot be considered just on its merits. It has to be also considered on its cost. We aren't opposed to new initiatives, especially on the middle school level, but someone has to pay the bills for those."[34]

The experience of these three schools in Denver underscores an important conclusion about Colorado's charter school program in the period covered by this study: while local school boards used their statutory authority to reject or modify charter proposals, they based their rejections and modifications only in the rarest cases on substantive educational issues. Resource issues predominated. In Colorado, applicants were often turned down altogether or urged to reduce the size (and thus the fiscal impact) of their schools or take less money per pupil.[35] But this study found no evidence that school districts in Colorado channeled charter school applicants down narrow educational paths. In this respect at least, Colorado's selection process resembled the processes in Massachusetts and Michigan.

Interviews with charter school applicants in all three states confirm this similarity. None of the 12 charter applicants reported any pressure, explicit or implicit, to modify their educational plans during the selection process. Applicants were urged to revise budgets, reduce student counts, and the like, but not to adopt different curriculums or pedagogy.[36] This cross-state similarity suggests that the threat posed to differentiation by the local school board's role lay more in restricting the number and size of charters than in restricting what charter schools do. It would not be much of an exaggeration to suggest that, according to the available record, local boards in Colorado were not much concerned with what charter schools did educationally. Their concerns revolved much more around the schools' impact on district finances.[37]

One way school districts could minimize the fiscal impact of charter schools is by focusing approval on schools serving students who are more expensive to educate, such as at-risk or special-needs children. Districts might actually realize a net financial gain if these students chose to attend charter schools. Combined with the fact that these students also tend to bring down district test-score averages, it would not be surprising to see districts allowing or even encouraging the creation of charter schools for at-risk children. Using this analysis, DPS might have looked particularly favorably on Clayton's application, since Clayton was committed to serving poor students in Denver. Aside from anecdotes like this one, however, there is not much evidence that Colorado districts disproportionately favored charter schools for the hard-to-educate. In fact, as Table 4-4 shows, very few of Colorado's first charter schools targeted at-risk students, and none targeted minority or special-needs children.

Operating Charter Schools

A charter school program's degree of differentiation begins with its selection process. But also critical is the regulatory regime under which charter schools work once they receive approval. A state with a very open selection process, for example, might limit differentiation by requiring charter schools to follow a narrow course after approval.

These four state charter laws differed in how much operating autonomy they extended to charter schools. Two dimensions of state legislation set the states apart: the degree of exemption from state law and regulation enjoyed by charter schools, and the legal and fiscal independence of charter schools as organizations. All four laws required charter schools to follow a core of state education law and regulation: charter schools could not charge tuition, admit students selectively, discriminate on the basis of race, sex, and other categories, or violate health and safety laws. Beyond those basic provisions, the four laws took different approaches to charter school exemptions. In Georgia and Colorado, schools were required to request waivers of state statutes and rules on a case-by-case basis. In both states, school districts could request waivers of state education laws and regulations. Since charter schools were legally part of school districts in both states, the procedure for petitioning for waivers was the same as for other public schools.[38]

In Michigan and Massachusetts, charter schools could not request specific exemptions. The Massachusetts charter law expressly exempted charter schools from state education law concerning the hiring, pay, and dismissal of staff, allowing charter schools to hire noncertified personnel, pay them as they pleased, and dismiss them at will. All other public school law applied, however. The Michigan charter law was similar but even more restrictive: all charter schools except those chartered by universities and community colleges were required to use certified teachers, and even schools chartered by institutions of higher education could only substitute their authorizers' faculty for certified teachers.

The other dimension of operating autonomy is the schools' legal and fiscal independence as organizations. In Michigan and Massachusetts, charter schools were authorized as independent government agencies. They could sue and be sued, own property, receive and disburse funds, enter into contracts, and exert other such powers. They received their funds directly from the state treasury on the basis of their student enrollment. Independence from local school districts in these states also meant that charter schools were not covered by collective-bargaining agreements between districts and unions. This exemption, perhaps more than many others, provided charter schools with great potential flexibility. In Colorado and Georgia, charter schools were part of the local school districts in which they operated. The law required Colorado's charter schools to have "governing bodies" that "administer and govern" the schools, but only "in a manner agreed to by the charter school applicant and the local board of education." Funds for charter schools flowed through local school districts in both states.

In other words, all four states' charter laws were complex. Charter schools in Massachusetts and Michigan lived in a relatively conventional legal regime, subject to most state laws and regulations. But they were legally and fiscally independent, answering to no local school boards.[39] Charter schools in Colorado and Georgia could in theory request all manner of waivers from state laws and regulations. Legally and fiscally, though, they were part of local school districts, not independent like their Massachusetts and Michigan counterparts. This mixed state of affairs points to the complexity of the idea of "autonomy." It also provides an opportunity to investigate the consequences of these different forms of freedom and constraint on the operation of charter schools.

This section considers how much autonomy charter schools enjoyed on four core elements of school management. The first, of course, is instruction: curriculum, pedagogy, the organization of time, the organization of students, and assessment. The second is staffing: whom to hire, how much and how to pay them, whom to dismiss. The third is organization and governance: the roles and duties of various members of the school community, including parents, teachers, administrators, students, and the governing board. The final element is finance: how schools spend their money.

The bottom line of the analysis is this: with the exception of Georgia, charter schools in these states reported a similarly wide range of latitude on these four elements, despite the large differences in the statutory framework of autonomy. In Colorado, Massachusetts, and Michigan, officials from all 11 schools interviewed reported virtually no interference from state or district officials on what or how they taught, how they dealt with their employees, how they organized and governed themselves, or how they spent money. As one principal put it: "We sit around in a room with a blank board and say: 'OK, how can we fit this puzzle together?' If it doesn't work, we'll go back to the drawing board and change things." Another remarked: "We have almost perfect freedom. We're not constrained on anything significant." Virtually all of those interviewed made similar comments.

How can these reports of wide latitude be squared with the apparent constraints under which charter schools operate—the relative lack of exemptions in Michigan and Massachusetts, the case-by-case waivering process, and the schools' lack of legal independence in Colorado? First, as in the case of the selection process, postadoption politics made possible in these three states a great deal of latitude for charter schools, even though the charter laws did not guarantee it. Second, many of the laws and regulations that did apply to charter schools are only loosely related to the core of educational practice. Though charter schools, like all public schools, were constrained in many ways, these constraints did not necessarily bind them on the four core elements of school decisionmaking listed above.

The Importance of Postadoption Politics

Colorado's charter law required charter schools to approach the state board of education with requests to waive any state law or regulation. Whether Colorado's law allowed charter schools to differentiate themselves significantly from conventional practice, then, depended largely on the state board's willingness to grant these waivers. If a majority of the state board believed that no public schools should be exempt from most state laws and regulations, charter schools would face much the same legal regime that regular public schools do. If, however, a majority of the state board favored giving charter schools the opportunity to work outside of major state laws and policies, differentiation would be enhanced. Since the state board is an elected body, politics played an important role in determining the degree of differentiation in Colorado's program.

From the outset, the majority of Colorado's state board favored differentiation. The board approved almost all requests for waivers brought before it. Almost all schools requested (and were granted) exemptions from many sections of Chapter 63, which governs teacher certification, hiring and firing, and pay; Chapter 32, which gives local school boards power over curriculum, personnel, and school finance; and Chapter 9, which requires teacher evaluations to be performed by duly certified principals.[40] The state board's orientation also helped charter schools achieve relative independence from their local school districts, even though they remained legally a part of them. Because the state board had shown itself to be willing to overturn local school boards' decisions, charter schools had more bargaining power at the local level and were able to negotiate quite a bit of independence from district policies and union contracts.

In Michigan and Massachusetts, state officials had no power to grant specific exemptions from laws and regulations, but postadoption politics were still important. Both states' laws required chartering authorities to sign contracts with charter schools specifying the terms under which the charter school would function. Because the laws granted a great deal of discretion to chartering authorities regarding the content of these contracts, the contract-writing process provided an opportunity for chartering authorities to reintroduce constraints that charter schools had hoped to escape. For example, although charter law in Massachusetts exempted schools from many personnel laws and regulations, contractual language could impose obligations that required schools to proceed in certain ways on personnel matters.

In practice, little of this sort of reregulation has occurred in either state. The Massachusetts contract was a simple legal boilerplate, the main provision of which was to incorporate by reference the school's charter application. The charter application, then, set out the obligations of the school. Since the application was written by school organizers, it did not reimpose any unwanted regulations.[41] The situation in Michigan was similar for schools chartered by Central Michigan University. CMU's contracts were more detailed than those in Massachusetts because they emphasized liability, reporting, and the like. The contracts did not place restrictions on the core elements of school management. As in Massachusetts, schools' primary contractual obligations on the core elements were contained in their charter applications, which they wrote themselves.[42]

The latitude enjoyed by schools in Colorado, Michigan, and Massachusetts, then, resulted largely from the orientation of those with authority to regulate charter schools. In all three states, top charter officials favored latitude, and so latitude prevailed. With a different balance of political power, the latitude enjoyed by charter schools in all three would likely have been narrower.

The Peripheral Emphasis of Law and Regulation

Though many state laws still applied to charter schools, these laws did not necessarily restrict charter schools' activities on the core elements of school management. In Massachusetts, Michigan, and Colorado, most of the prescriptive law and regulation that applied to charter schools related primarily to more peripheral aspects of schooling.[43] An examination of Massachusetts illustrates this point.

In Massachusetts, there was very little regulation of curriculum and instruction at the state level. [44] State education law tended to be broad in its prescriptions, such as this statement about what students should learn:

> Such schools shall be taught by teachers of competent ability and good morals, and shall give instruction and training in orthography, reading, writing, the English language and grammar, geography, arithmetic, drawing, music, the history and Constitution of the United States, the duties of citizenship, health education, physical education, and good behavior.[45]

Other sections of the code stated that schools should teach the history of Massachusetts; that "motor vehicle driving education may be incorporated"; that schools "may include instruction by means of [televised] educational programs"; and that principals shall select textbooks subject to school district direction.[46] These provisions did not give schools complete discretion over what to teach, but most would not regard them as heavily prescriptive. Within these broad guidelines, public schools (including charter schools) had a fair amount of latitude over the first core element of schooling.[47]

On the second core element, staffing, charter schools were made exempt from most significant state law. On the third, organization and governance, Massachusetts law left these matters primarily to local school districts. Since charter schools were independent of local districts, they faced no constraints in this area beyond the requirements in the charter law that the schools' curriculum and budget be set by their boards of trustees in consultation with their teachers. On the fourth element, school finance, Massachusetts had an elaborate set of formulas that determined how much schools received. But the state placed very few restrictions on how the recipients (school districts or charter schools) spent the money. In fact, the law stated: "Except as required by general law, each school district may determine how to allocate any funds appropriated for the support of public schools."[48] "General law" did impose some restrictions, such as requirements for competitive bidding on major purchases, but largely left school districts (and thus charter schools) free to allocate funds as they saw fit.[49]

To be sure, many aspects of the commonwealth's school law were quite restrictive and applicable to charter schools. But these laws tended either not to regulate the core elements of schooling at all or to regulate them just for subgroups of students rather than the general population. Charter schools were required to file reams of reports, ensure the safety of facilities, adhere to health codes, hold open meetings, and respect the rights of students. Though some charter schools regarded these restrictions as burdensome, they did not, for the most part, constrain charter schools in what they taught and how they taught it, whom they hired and fired, how they organized and governed themselves, and how they spent their money; in short, these laws did not constrain charter schools on the core elements of schooling. Laws and regulations regarding special and bilingual education did, however, go to the heart of these core elements, restricting educational offerings, staffing, decisionmaking processes, and spending. But they did so only for a small fraction of the student population, leaving charter schools free to control the core elements for the great majority of their students.[50]

In Michigan, Massachusetts, and Colorado, the confluence of postadoption politics and public school law created an environment in which charter schools enjoyed great latitude on the core elements of school management. But the situation in Georgia was markedly different. As required by law, all three charter schools in Georgia were converted public schools. And all three had specific motives for seeking charter status: they wanted minor exemptions from state law or district policy. Otherwise, one principal remarked in an interview, "everything is exactly the same" as it was before charter status.[51] Thus Georgia's schools did not report the same kind of operating latitude that schools in the other states reported.

Discussion

In all four states, legislatures struck political compromises that threatened the autonomy of charter schools. In Georgia these compromises

were particularly severe, and they greatly influenced the degree of differentiation achieved by the state's charter program. On all three measures
of differentiation discussed in this chapter, Georgia achieved less than
the other three states. Charter schools in Georgia proliferated less quickly,
exhibited less diversity, and enjoyed less operating autonomy on the core
elements of school management than their counterparts in the other
states. Georgia's experience emerges as a textbook case of a program
saddled by compromise-induced constraints that made it virtually impossible to succeed.

Experience in the other three states was more complicated. Though
written with fewer compromises than Georgia's law, charter statutes in
Colorado, Massachusetts, and Michigan all contained autonomy-threatening provisions. But despite these constraints, and despite the consid-
erable differences between the states, charter programs in all three states
exhibited similarly high levels of differentiation on the three measures
examined here. Most notably, charter schools in all three states reported
high levels of operating autonomy, citing their freedom to set curriculum and pedagogy, choose staff, organize and govern themselves, and
spend money. All three states also chartered schools whose size, instructional approach, and target population differed widely. The proliferation of schools was rapid by national charter school standards,[52] though
charter schools still comprised a small fraction of the school population
in all three states.

Clearly, the relative lack of compromise made an important difference. Access to nonlocal bodies for approval introduced great potential
for differentiation into the selection process. And in Massachusetts and
Michigan at least, independence from local school boards meant freedom from local district policies and union contracts. Without these legislative provisions, charter schools would have found the environment
much more restrictive.

But two other factors also proved critical. First, postadoption politics
in all three states worked in favor of differentiation, minimizing the importance of legislative restrictions. Second, those constraints that charter schools did face tended not to restrict them on the four core elements
of school management. One reason charter schools in these states enjoyed such wide latitude on school operations is that the laws and regu-

lations to which they were subject tended either not to relate to these core elements or to constrain them only in reference to small subgroups of students. The laws and regulations most applicable to charter schools often had to do with activities at the periphery of schooling: reporting requirements, building codes, financial procedures, and the like; they were nuisances, perhaps, but they did not interfere with schools' ability to set curriculum, devise instructional practices, choose staff, organize and govern themselves, or allocate funds. When they did constrain charter schools in the core, they did so for special-education students, bilingual-education students, or other small subgroups, not for the general population. So while charter schools faced a larger-than-expected burden of regulation, they remained relatively autonomous in their core operations.

To be sure, state law and regulation did directly address one important element of the core: staffing. In all three states general school law included requirements concerning the hiring of certified staff, the conditions under which and procedures by which schools could dismiss employees, and, to a lesser extent, salaries. In Massachusetts the law explicitly exempted charter schools from most of these restrictions. In Colorado, charter schools requested and received waivers from the state board.

These exemptions, like the evidence on importance of postadoption politics, indicate the limited importance of legislative compromise. Even under the burden of substantial regulation, charter schools were free to conduct school business more or less as they pleased. This outcome brings to mind the sociological literature on "loose coupling" in educational organizations, which says that educational organizations engage in a range of "ceremonial" behaviors, some imposed by law, others inculcated through socialization.[53] These rituals are only loosely related, if related at all, to the technical activities of educational organizations, which carry on more or less unconstrained. The regulations followed by charter schools in these states had this ceremonial quality: they required the filing of required reports, the preparation of written individual education plans for special-education children, submission to inspections and audits, and adherence to open-meetings laws. These activities, though time-consuming, had little impact on schools' conduct of the core technical activities of schooling and thus little impact on the most important work of charter schools.

Does this mean that political compromises on these issues were of no consequence and that legislative concessions mattered only in Georgia? To answer that question, we need to move beyond the issue of differentiation. Legislative compromises may not have placed many limits on differentiation in Colorado, Massachusetts, and Michigan. But they may have had other consequences for the potential of charter school programs in these states. The next chapter turns to a second indicator of charter school programs' promise: the degree to which they enable charter schools to be viable as organizations.

5 | *Open for Business*

THE POSSIBILITY of school failure is fundamental to the charter school idea. If charter schools cannot attract enough students to cover their costs, or if they do not live up to the terms of their contracts, they lose their charters. This possibility of failure constitutes the real teeth of the "accountability" side of the bargain into which charter schools enter. In exchange for the freedom to be different, they agree to be judged by both the market and the public agencies that monitor the achievement of their students.

For a charter school program to work, though, the schools must at least be able to stay in business if they succeed at attracting students and meeting their goals. If charter schools that are successful in these ways cannot make ends meet, the programs cannot have the impact that their proponents envision. Charter schools, provided they meet the tests of the market and the evaluators, must be financially viable as organizations.

One way in which legislative compromise might hamper the effectiveness of charter school programs is by threatening the institutional viability of charter schools. A charter school law might pose such a threat by providing inadequate resources to charter schools. Or it might do so by imposing excessive costs. Either way, deals made in legislatures might make it difficult for charter schools to survive as "businesses," even if they attract "customers" and satisfy their regulators.

This chapter explores the question of the viability of charter schools in three steps. First, it considers in general terms the financial challenges facing charter schools, setting out a simple analytical framework for examining the cost and revenue structure of charter school operation. Second, in light of that framework it explores ways in which state charter legislation might endanger the financial viability of charter schools. Third, it presents evidence from the four states on how charter schools have fared as businesses.

There is substantial evidence that legislative compromises have had a negative impact on the financial fortunes of charter schools. Legislative provisions that restrict the range of potential charter operators, impose regulatory burdens on charter schools, and provide inadequate or poorly timed funding have made it difficult for schools to make ends meet. But two additional factors confound this straightforward link between compromise and suboptimal results. First, most of charter schools' financial difficulties have arisen not from legislative compromise but from legislative success in obtaining independence and autonomy for charter schools. Independence emerges as a double-edged sword, allowing charter schools the flexibility to innovate but endangering their institutional viability. Second, legislation has not been the end of the story. Almost all charter schools have managed, despite formidable challenges, to make ends meet financially. Though legislation set parameters within which charter schools worked, their actions within those constraints had a large effect on outcomes.

The Financial Challenges Facing Charter Schools

Before examining schools' actual experiences, I provide a general picture of the financial world in which charter schools function. This section considers charter schools' costs and revenues.

Costs

All charter schools have startup costs and ongoing expenses. Startup costs are highest for start-from-scratch institutions: those that come into existence for the first time as charter schools. But even charter schools that convert from existing public or private schools face some conversion costs. By far the most significant startup expense is the cost of a facility. Schooling requires specialized space, and real estate that is school-ready is scarce in most places. Other space is potentially usable, but substantial and costly renovations are typically required to bring a nonschool building (such as a warehouse, an office building, or retail space) up to the specifications of school building codes. The costs of readying a facility can range from a few thousand dollars for small cosmetic improvements to millions of dollars for major construction or renovation.

Though facilities costs tend to dwarf other startup expenses, staffing is also expensive. Because it will not do for school staff to begin work on the same day that the students arrive, schools need to hire at least part-time leadership well before opening, and to bring on a close-to-full staff nearer to, but still before, the arrival of students. Schools may also need to contract with specialized consultants for various aspects of their preparation. Another major expense is equipment and supplies. When school opens, institutions need everything from desks and chairs to pencils and chalk to computers and telephone systems. They must also recruit a student body, find staff members, train employees, set up an accounting system, and the like, all of which involve some up-front spending.

Once charter schools are open, their ongoing expenses resemble those of regular public schools. Namely, almost all funds go to pay the salaries and benefits of staff or contract employees. The primary difference between a charter school's budget and that of a regular public school is the charter school's independence from a school district. In most school systems, individual public schools do not receive lump-sum payments that they use to pay for staff, supplies, transportation, upkeep of facilities, and the like. Instead, central school district bureaucracies expend these funds on behalf of individual schools. School administrators may receive some discretionary funds, but these tend to be a small percentage of the total school budget.

Because charter schools are not part of local school districts (at least in the ideal model), their spending is not handled by a central district office. Fiscal independence has both a negative and a positive impact. On the negative side, charter schools lack economies of scale. They tend to be smaller than conventional public schools, and more to the point, they are almost always smaller than public school *districts*. Because they are independent, charter schools are often treated as if they are school districts: they are required to provide the same level of services to special-needs children, file the same reports, meet the same requirements for financial and program audits, and manage and maintain their facilities. As small "districts," charter schools have fewer students over which to spread the costs of these activities. And they have more difficulty than school districts arranging for lower-cost bulk purchases. Their per-pupil costs, then, tend to be higher than those of conventional school districts.[1]

On the positive side, charter schools have flexibility to spend their money as they see fit. Even though they cannot spread their costs over as many students, they are more free than conventional schools to allocate funds. Whereas regular schools might have to adhere to rigid salary schedules, charter schools may be able to design systems of compensation that meet their unique needs. Whereas conventional districts may be obligated by contract to use employees to perform some duty, charter schools might be free to contract out the service. If charter schools take advantage of this flexibility to cut costs, they can compensate for their lack of economies of scale.

Revenues

Charter schools' primary source of revenue is the public purse. Though state funding formulas vary widely, they are designed to provide a "fair share" of public funds for each student in a charter school. Since school funds are typically a mix of federal, state, and local revenue streams, and since some these streams depend on such factors as the socioeconomic status or special needs of individual students, funding calculations can become complicated. But in theory, they are designed to provide a charter school with the average per-pupil cost of the school district in which each of its students resides, adjusted for characteristics of the student body.

In practice, per-pupil funds may not meet the needs of charter schools, for two reasons. First, because per-pupil funds typically do not begin to flow until students arrive in the fall, or perhaps even after that, schools in their first year of operation must finance all of the startup costs with revenues other than their per-pupil dollars, whether borrowed or received as donations. Furthermore, even after per-pupil dollars begin flowing, cash-flow problems may persist if payments lag (in time) behind expenses. Second, if charter schools receive only operating money but must also pay for facilities (as most state charter laws require), their per-pupil dollars will fall short. And if the lack of economies of scale outweighs the cost-gains charter schools achieve through flexibility, even receiving the true average per-pupil costs will not be adequate. Thus charter schools may have to look to resources other than public revenues. _____

The Expected Importance of Legislation

With an understanding of charter school financing in mind, it becomes clear how legislative compromises might affect charter schools' ability to make ends meet.

Who Can Open a Charter School

A law that requires all charter schools to be conversions of existing public schools eliminates many (though not all) startup expenses. Most important, such a law allows schools to begin their new lives with facilities and equipment. A law that allows private schools to assume charter status might have the same effect. In the four states in this study, Georgia's law allowed only public school conversions. Michigan's allowed both public and private school conversions. Laws in both Massachusetts and Colorado allowed public school conversions but disallowed private school conversions.

The Regulatory Regime

How much freedom charter schools enjoy from legal and regulatory requirements might prove important in two respects. First, complying with high regulatory burdens is costly, especially since charter schools have to spread the costs of compliance over fewer students than a typical school district. Second, to the extent that regulations restrict the flexibility of charter schools, they may limit the schools' ability to compensate for the lack of economies of scale by spending funds creatively. In Colorado and Georgia, charter schools could seek waivers from most state law and regulation, but the state board of education had to agree. In Michigan and Massachusetts, most state law applied, though charter schools automatically received a few key exemptions. In all the states, federal law and regulation of course applied fully to charter schools.

Legal Independence

As noted above, independence is a double-edged sword. In Colorado and Georgia, charter schools were legally part of local school districts. In Massachusetts and Michigan, they were independent public agencies.

The Funding Stream

One possible legislative compromise is to provide charter schools with less-than-average per-pupil funds. Legislation might exclude certain types of funding (most commonly money for facilities) from the formula by which per-pupil costs are calculated, or offer charter schools less than 100 percent of per-pupil costs, however calculated. In Massachusetts, charter schools received 100 percent of per-pupil operating funds from each student's home district plus whatever federal entitlement funds attached to the charter schools' students, but not state capital funds. In Michigan, charter schools received 100 percent of the state per-pupil funding for each student's home district, which in Michigan constitutes most of school operating money, plus federal entitlements, but not capital funding. In Colorado and Georgia, schools had to negotiate funding with their school districts. In Colorado, districts were required to provide at least 80 percent of per-pupil operating revenue (PPOR); but in that state 80 percent of PPOR amounts to only about 52 percent of total district spending.[2] Georgia's charter law did not dictate what districts had to provide.

Table 5-1. *Characteristics of Michigan Charter Schools, 1995–96*

Characteristics	Mean	Minimum	Median	Maximum
Number of pupils	122	8	102.3	390
Per-pupil expenditures	$5,769	$2,590	$5,455	$9,739
Per-pupil revenues	$6,320	$4,224	$5,769	$9,678
Per-pupil surplus (deficit)	$551	($2,040)	$366	$3,173
Number of schools with a surplus	29 of 37	. . .	. . .	. . .
Number of schools starting from scratch in 1995–96	23 of 37	. . .	. . .	. . .
Number of schools converted from private schools	10 of 37	. . .	. . .	. . .

Source: Michigan Department of Education, *A Description of Michigan Public School Academies: 1995–96 Report to the House and Senate Committees in Education* (Lansing, 1996).

Evidence from the States

How have charter schools fared financially in the four states under study? For data, the analysis draws on two sets of sources. The state department of education in Michigan compiled financial information on 37 of the 41 charter schools, including their total revenues and expenses for the 1995–96 school year (see Table 5-1). Though helpful, this information paints the financial picture of charter schools in fairly broad strokes, and does so for only one state. In addition, I conducted interviews with officials of three to five randomly selected charter schools and other knowledgeable individuals in all four states and obtained detailed financial records from some individual schools. Press reports from each state provided supplemental information.

Starting Up

The Michigan state department of education does not categorize expenses as startup and ongoing. But it is possible to use the Michigan data to compare the financial fortunes of start-from-scratch schools with those of pre-existing schools. In 1995–96, ten of the 37 charter schools in the Michigan data set were converted private schools. Another four schools

Table 5-2. *Comparison of Finances of Start-from-Scratch and Existing Schools, 1995–96*

Dollars

Type of school	Mean per pupil		
	Revenues	*Expenses*	*Surplus*
Start-from-scratch	6,431	5,942	489
Pre-existing	6,138	5,485	652
Difference	293	457	−163

Source: Michigan Department of Education, *Description of Michigan Public School Academies.*

had been open as charter schools in the previous school year. The rest, 23 schools, started from scratch in the fall of 1995. Table 5-2 compares the finances of start-from-scratch with pre-existing schools in 1995–96.

The per-pupil expenses of start-from-scratch schools in Michigan were higher than those of their pre-existing counterparts by over 8 percent.[3] To be sure, it is impossible based on these data alone to attribute this difference solely to these schools' startup status. If start-from-scratch schools served disproportionately disadvantaged students or operated in areas with high costs of living, their per-pupil expenditures could be higher even if startup costs were not a burden. But another possibility is that start-from-scratch schools carried the costs of starting up into the first year of their operations. Perhaps they borrowed money before opening and were paying it back during their first year of operation. Perhaps they delayed important startup purchases (new equipment or staff training) until state aid began to flow in the fall of 1995. At least some portion of the $457 differential observed here may be due to the financial burdens of starting up.

The typical start-from-scratch school was still in the black in 1995–96, with a mean surplus of $489. Some 74 percent of start-from-scratch schools and 86 percent of pre-existing schools showed surpluses. But even this somewhat positive outcome arose only because start-from-scratch schools received higher per-pupil revenues than their pre-existing peers. If start-from-scratch schools' revenue had equaled the median per-pupil revenue of pre-existing schools, only 13 (57 percent) would have been solvent.

This quantitative evidence was confirmed in part by school officials. Of the 15 schools where I conducted interviews, three were converted private schools (two in Michigan and one in Colorado), and three were converted public schools (all in Georgia). The others were start-from-scratch institutions. To be sure, all school officials mentioned difficulties they faced in the startup phase of their operations. All in all, however, the troubles cited by start-from-scratch schools centered much more on financial issues than those cited by converted schools. Similarly, in a 1998 national survey of charter schools, officials in newly created charter schools were much more likely to cite lack of startup funds and somewhat more likely to cite inadequate operating funds than those in conversion charter schools. Even in converted schools, however, resource limitations topped the list of reported challenges.[4]

For the converted schools I examined for this book, the primary difficulties had to do with the added responsibilities they had to take on as quasi-public charter schools, though the changes differed for private and public school conversions. For private schools, the conversion to charter school entailed adhering to a body of public law that previously had not applied to them. Two schools cited difficulties assuming their duty to transport students to school, something they had previously left to parents. All three noted the magnitude of the task of learning what laws did and did not apply to them as charter schools. While these complications "cost" staff time, they did not require the financial outlays that start-from-scratch schools had to incur. In fact, the finances of all three private schools improved as a result of converting to charter status, since the state aid they received exceeded their average actual tuition payments as private schools and increased their enrollment without proportionately increasing their costs.[5] The public school conversions in Georgia were less difficult since (as noted in the previous chapter) Georgia's charter law allows so little differentiation on the part of charter schools. One school, though, mentioned that it was difficult to make time for the planning required by the charter law while running an existing school. This, perhaps, is the one sense in which start-from-scratch schools had an advantage over their pre-existing counterparts: they did not have to create their charter schools while operating an educational institution full time.

Start-from-scratch schools, though, focused heavily on the financial strains of starting new schools. Financing a facility ranked at the top of the list of startup problems for most of the nine start-from-scratch schools in the study. For many, the difficulty began simply with finding a suitable facility. In a given town, especially a small one, there are likely to be only a few possible spaces. In Colorado, one school resorted to using portable modular classroom units donated to the school and placed on land leased from a church. In Massachusetts, only nine of the 14 schools slated to open in the fall of 1994 had lined up space by the preceding March. Two other schools scheduled to open in fall 1995 delayed their launches for one year on account of problems finding space.[6] One school opened using a motel as temporary space, and students took recess in the parking lot.[7] All five Massachusetts school administrators interviewed for this project had difficulty finding a place to set up shop, though all did eventually.[8] In Michigan, at least one school failed to open at all in the fall of 1995 in part because it could not find a facility.[9]

Once they had secured facilities, the schools faced the task of bringing them up to stringent school building codes in time for school to open. In Colorado, one school had to find $30,000 just to meet the requirements for changing the building's classification from "church" to "school." Another facility was still not up to code when opening day rolled around. The school operated for its first days in unfinished space in the public library. In Massachusetts, one school learned that the site it had selected had extensive fuel and phosphate contamination.[10] Another found a building, but then discovered $1 million worth of asbestos removal would be required.[11] That school scuttled its plans to start altogether, citing the lack of a facility as the primary reason. One school interviewed for this study found a former university building but was able to bring it into shape only with the help of a low-interest loan from the state.[12]

Though facilities costs were the most significant startup expense, the fledgling institutions had other expenses as well before opening. Table 5-3 summarizes information from the annual report of City on a Hill charter school in Boston. This 65-student school spent $73,000 on nonfacilities startup costs. Though each school had a slightly different startup experience, this school's costs were roughly comparable to those of other schools in the study, approximately $1,000 per pupil.

Table 5-3. *Nonfacilities Startup Costs for City on a Hill Charter School*
Dollars

Item	Amount
Capital equipment	29,825
Payroll	14,423
Technology consultant	7,662
Fundraising	14,344
Administration	2,462
Professional development	1,215
Recruitment of students	1,735
Recruitment of faculty	1,390
Total	73,056
	(1,124 per pupil)

Source: City on a Hill Charter School, *Annual Report 1995–96* (Boston, 1996), p. 23.

Equipment and staffing require the biggest financial outlays. New schools have to furnish their facilities with everything from desks and chalkboards to library books and shelves to computers and office equipment. They have to hire and train staff (or consultants) before school opens. Charter school officials listed numerous other time-consuming tasks that occupied them in the months before opening: advertising and filling teaching positions; marketing their schools to prospective students and their families; conducting a selection process; fleshing out the curriculum and instructional strategies; learning about the laws and regulations to which all public schools, including charter schools, are subject; acquiring equipment and furniture; and finding contractors and negotiating contracts for food service, custodial services, special-education administration, bilingual education, and renovation of facilities.

Operating Costs

Once charter schools are open, their operating costs resemble those of any other school. But the typically smaller charter schools have to perform all of the duties of regular schools, as well as some of the duties of school districts, without the economies of scale regular schools and

Table 5-4. *Michigan Charter Schools, by Enrollment and Spending Level, 1995–96*

	Smaller schools	*Larger schools*
Lower-spending schools	10	9
Higher-spending schools	9	9

Source: Michigan Department of Education, *Description of Michigan Public School Academies.*

districts enjoy. Thus their per-pupil costs may be higher than those of regular schools. Against that, charter schools should be able to use their freedom to spend money as they see fit to reduce their unit costs.

Ideally, one would compare financial data on the costs of regular public schools with those of charter schools. Unfortunately, most conventional public schools do not budget and record expenditures at the school level.[13] To examine the question of economies of scale, though, it is possible to compare the financial circumstances of smaller charter schools with those of larger charter schools. The Michigan data set makes such a comparison possible. Among the 37 schools that reported financial data, one had only 8 students; another had 390; the median was 102.3. Did the smaller schools in this group face higher per-pupil costs than the larger schools?

In the aggregate, the answer is no. There is no apparent relationship between per-pupil expenditures and enrollment (see Figure 5-1 and Table 5-4). And if one divides schools into two groups—those with enrollment at or below the median and those with enrollment above the median—per-pupil spending in 1995–96 was actually slightly higher in the larger schools ($5,662) than in the smaller schools ($5,418).

As with the comparison of startup with pre-existing schools, this analysis does not allow the definitive conclusion that larger and smaller charter schools do not differ in their cost structures. Since most charter schools in Michigan are nonprofits, they have no real incentive to minimize costs. Per-pupil expenditures, then, may have been driven more by the availability of revenues than by the underlying costs of the schools. In addition, small and large schools may have differed in ways other than their size that affect costs. For example, larger schools in areas with higher costs of living may have had higher per-pupil costs despite the econo-

Figure 5-1. *Enrollment and per-Pupil Costs in Michigan Charter Schools, 1995–96*

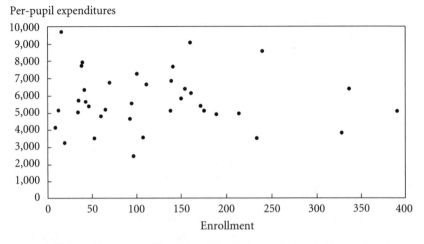

Per-pupil expenditures

Enrollment

Source: Michigan Department of Education, *A Description of Michigan Public School Academies: 1995–96 Report to the House and Senate Committees in Education* (Lansing, 1996).

mies of scale they enjoyed. Finally, the range of school sizes in this data set (from 8 to 390 students) is still much smaller than that of regular public schools. It is possible that all 37 schools had access to (or lack) comparable economies of scale.

More anecdotal evidence from the interviews suggests that at least in some specific areas, the lack of economies of scale made a difference to charter schools, particularly in special education. In all the states in this study, charter schools are required to provide special-education services for students in accordance with the students' individualized education plans, or IEPs. This requirement includes: (1) the cost of testing students to determine their needs; (2) the cost of developing the tailored IEPs in response to the tests; (3) the cost of delivering the services demanded by the IEP; (4) the cost of complying with procedural regulations regarding documentation, reporting, and decisionmaking; and (5) the cost of legal counsel to advise schools in these matters and, in extreme cases, to defend schools in lawsuits.[14] In each area the opportunities for economies of scale are clear. School districts can hire specialized staff in most of these areas to handle the cases of many students. And school districts can bring students with similar needs together in classrooms (or at least in schools) by hiring certified personnel and purchasing appropriate equipment.

Charter schools cannot obtain such scale economies without going outside their own walls. Someone on the school staff must develop at least enough expertise to supervise consultants who carry out the work. And charter schools must provide the full range of required services to an eligible student, even if that student is the only one with a particular set of needs. As a result, the per-pupil cost of providing special-education services can be very high in charter schools. Virtually every charter school interviewed for this study (with the exception of those in Georgia, which are still part of school districts) cited special education as one area where their inability to achieve economies of scale affected their costs markedly.

Charter schools also cited lack of economies of scale in fulfilling reporting requirements. In Massachusetts, charter schools were required to collect data for and prepare three types of reports: reports required of all public schools, reports required of charter schools alone, and reports required of all school districts (since charter schools are in effect small school districts) (see Table 5-5). As with special education, this data collection, analysis, and reporting required dedicated staff. Since charter schools could spread the cost of staff time only over smaller numbers of students, their per-pupil reporting costs were higher, especially for district-level reports.

These two examples, special education and reporting requirements, also highlight another important point about the ongoing costs of charter schools. As noted above, charter schools can, in theory, compensate for their lack of access to scale economies by exercising cost-saving flexibility in their expenditures, due to the exemptions they receive from laws and regulations. But to the extent that regular public school restrictions apply to charter schools, as they do for special education and reporting, charter schools have little opportunity to reduce costs.

The previous chapter showed that charter schools in three of the four states in this study (Georgia being the exception) enjoyed wide latitude to chart their own courses on the four core elements of school management: curriculum and instruction, staffing, organization and governance, and spending. But on more peripheral issues (like reporting) and rules

Table 5-5. *Charter School Reporting Requirements in Massachusetts*

Reports required of charter schools as public schools
　Individual school report (enrollment by grade, race, sex, residence, language, income)
　Education reform school staff report (staffing by race, gender, tenure)
　Student exclusion reports (filed if student is expelled or suspended for ten days)
　Returned dropout report
　Nutrition report (if participating in national school lunch or breakfast programs)
　School choice enrollment report
　Special education: federal child count reports and special education exit reports
　Education reform act capacity report (projected seats and enrollment for next year)
　Year-end school indicators report; end of year pupil and financial report

Reports required of charter schools as school districts
　Foundation enrollment (students enrolled by grade, language, income)
　School system summary (staff by certification, language)
　Education reform system staff report
　Science and math indicators (enrollment and staff information on math and science courses)

Reports required of charter schools as charter schools
　Annual report to parents and state
　Enrollment reports to state for funding purposes

Source: Emily Nielsen Jones, "Reports Required of Charter Schools," memorandum to charter schools, Boston: Massachusetts Executive Office of Education, September 25, 1995.

that applied to subgroups of students (like special education), charter schools were highly constrained. Because they sidestepped the core of schooling of the majority of the students, these constraints did not appear to prevent charter schools from implementing their innovative educational designs. This does mean, however, that these constraints had no negative impact on charter schools. According to charter school officials, the primary effect of restrictions like these was to raise charter schools' operating costs. Two additional examples illustrate this point.

　One charter school devised a cost-saving way to provide food service. Its plan would have provided each student with a debit card for use at a nearby university-based food center. The school proposed to add funds directly to the debit cards of students entitled to reduced-price or free lunches. Other students would add their own funds as they wished. The technology would have allowed the school to limit the students' purchases to certain foods—for example, pupils could have been prevented from making a full lunch out of candy bars. The plan appealed to school officials because it allowed the school to make lunch available to students at minimal cost to the school: no caterer to hire and supervise, no school space required, and so forth. The scheme, however, ran afoul not of state law but of federal requirements for the reduced-price lunch program, which mandated more direct school control of lunch offerings. As a result, the school had to contract directly with a food-service provider to make lunch available at school, incurring all of the costs it had hoped to avoid.

Another school proposed that teachers serve as van drivers to transport children, which would have eliminated the need to hire or contract for bus drivers. But state school-safety law, to which all charter schools are subject, prohibited this practice, forcing the school to adopt a more expensive arrangement.

In these instances the public school rules and regulations prevented charter schools from using their financial flexibility to achieve cost savings and thus to overcome the problems arising from their small size.

Revenues

Most revenue for charter schools in these states came from public sources. In Michigan and Massachusetts, charter schools received for each enrolled student an amount approximating the per-pupil costs incurred by that student's home school district. In Colorado, charter schools negotiated a per-pupil funding amount with their school districts. In Georgia, charter schools remained administratively part of their school districts, and their expenses were paid in the same manner as those of conventional public schools. In all states, charter schools received federal funds based on the number of students in certain categories.

As noted above, two potential problems arose regarding these public revenues: inadequacy and poor timing. On the question of adequacy, for 24 of the schools, the Michigan data set includes the amount of state aid

Table 5-6. *Revenues for Michigan Charter Schools, 1995–96*[a]

Dollars unless otherwise specified

Revenues	Mean	Minimum	Median	Maximum
Total per-pupil revenues	6,309	4,224	5,921	9,370
Per-pupil state aid	5,320	3,909	5,471	6,077
Per-pupil nonstate funds	989	0	509	4,013
State aid as a portion of revenues (percent)	87	57	91	100

Source: General revenue figures from Michigan Department of Education, *Description of Michigan Public School Academies.* State aid figures from Central Michigan University Resource Center for Charter Schools, *Annual Report Period Ending June 30, 1996* (Mt. Pleasant, 1996).

a. Data available for only 24 schools.

received by charter schools, a number that is distinct from total revenues (see Table 5-6). On average, $6,309 flowed into these schools for every student. Of that, $5,320 came from the state, the remaining $989 from other sources. Four schools received all their funding from the state; five received less than 75 percent. The rest obtained somewhere between three-quarters and all their funding from the state.

The most important figure is the average amount of per-pupil nonstate funds raised by these schools, $989, which exceeds the average per-pupil surplus by $548. In other words, the average school would have been in the red without the infusion of nonstate funds. Indeed, though only 7 of the 24 schools were in the red with all their revenues considered, more than twice as many, 15, would have found themselves with a deficit if only state funds had been available. Data on Massachusetts are more limited and not strictly comparable but paint much the same picture. Schools received an average of $780 per pupil from private donations, about 12 percent of overall expenditures.[15]

It is important to note that these shortfalls occurred in Michigan and Massachusetts, where the funding formulas for charter schools were relatively generous. Contrast these systems, in which schools received close to the full per-pupil revenue available in their areas, with Colorado's, in which funding was negotiable. Colorado's law required districts to provide charter schools with at least 80 percent of per-pupil operating revenues. But PPOR itself represented only a fraction of school district spending. In the 1993–94 school year, the average PPOR was $4,214. But districts spent $6,476 on average. Eighty percent of PPOR ($3,371) represented just 52 percent of overall per-pupil spending.[16]

Since each charter school had to work out an individual arrangement with its school district, actual funding for charter schools in Colorado varied greatly from school to school. Many schools received 80–90 percent of PPOR. In theory, they also received services from the district that added up to the remainder of the per-pupil allotment. At the other extreme was Douglas County, a fast-growing district just south of Denver, in which schools received 100 percent of PPOR. They could then choose to purchase services from the district at cost on a per-pupil basis. The district developed a schedule of services, each with a per-pupil cost. But schools were also free to contract with other providers of those services.[17] Even in Douglas County, though, 100 percent of PPOR still fell short of per-pupil spending. If Michigan schools had difficulty making ends meet with their primary source of funds, it stands to reason that Colorado schools were even more stretched. Interviews with charter schools in Colorado support this hypothesis, though one school in the study had such large private subsidies that it was not financially strained.

Though adequacy is clearly a primary issue in charter school funding, a second potential difficulty is timing. None of the revenues discussed so far began to flow until the schools opened their doors to educate students (or later). Schools incurred all of the startup expenses discussed above before receiving any funding. So even if funding was adequate to cover ongoing expenses, almost every charter school interviewed for this study reported difficulty covering costs in that interim period.

Coping

How did charter schools deal with these financial issues? Each school's experience was slightly different, but five approaches to obtaining and managing money were common to all of them: obtaining federal funding for startup costs; obtaining private funding for startup and operational costs; mobilizing volunteer efforts; joining forces with trade associations or "resource centers"; and contracting with school districts for services.

First, charter schools in all four states received substantial startup funding from the federal government through a special grant program. States with charter school programs are eligible to apply to the U.S. Department of Education for grants, 95 percent of which they must then distribute to charter schools. Each charter school in this study received between $20,000 and $50,000 in grants through this program.

Second, charter schools raised substantial sums from private sources. As noted above, private donations to charter schools in Massachusetts totaled more than $2 million in 1995–96, about $780 for each student.[18] Aggregate data are not available for the other states, but every school in the study reported raising donations from private individuals, companies, or foundations. Where the federal grants were distributed relatively evenly among schools, private fundraising yielded more resources for some schools than for others. One school in Michigan received a grant from a single foundation totaling $300,000, which alone constituted more than 10 percent of the total nonstate funds received by the 24 Michigan charter schools for which we have the data. As noted above, four Michigan schools received *all* of their funding from the state in 1995–96; four others received 99 percent or more from the state. One school in Colorado pledged in its budget to supplement an expected public contribution of $870,000 over three years with $1.42 million in private funds, matching public dollars 1.6 to 1. Another raised $152,995 in grants and donations in 1995–96, constituting 37 percent of its budget.

Third, schools reported an extraordinary amount of volunteer time donated by board members, parents, students, and community supporters. Volunteer effort was most intense in the startup phase; using volunteers to perform major functions was one of the primary ways charter schools dealt with the fact that funds would not flow until school opened. As one charter school annual report notes, volunteers fixed the building's roof, cleaned and painted the facility, provided legal advice, printed letterhead and business cards, and raised money.[19] In other schools volunteers designed instructional programs, recruited staff and students, and helped the schools negotiate contracts for key services.[20]

Most schools continued to welcome volunteer efforts after opening. At P.S. 1 volunteers performed tasks as diverse as tutoring, chaperoning outings, office work, conducting school surveys, orienting new families, and planning events. In one school, parent and community volunteers staffed the kitchen, and students performed most routine janitorial tasks. Another set aside a special room in the school for parent volunteers, four or five of whom were at the school at any one time. Another recruited community members to serve as judges for student presentations, which were a critical part of the school's assessment of its students' progress. All the schools interviewed for the study had active boards of trustees, who contributed to everything from curriculum design to fundraising to setting policies.

Teachers and other staff also took on unconventional roles in the operation of the school. As one school principal and founder recounted, numerous tasks arise in the process of opening a school that do not fall into anyone's job description, such as purchasing equipment for and setting up the computer lab, devising the school's code of conduct for students, and arranging for special-education services. Without funding for a full-time technology coordinator, an assistant principal responsible for discipline, or a special-education administrator, this principal had to ask individual teachers to take on these jobs. Often, the teachers turned to outside consultants (paid or volunteer) for technical expertise. But ultimate responsibility for the tasks fell to the teachers. In most schools this practice often meant longer hours and steep learning curves for staff. But it was another way in which schools made ends meet, especially in the startup phase.

Fourth, schools came to rely on statewide associations and resource organizations to share or reduce costs in all the states except Georgia. Michigan has the most well-developed support network of the four states. Early in the process, the Michigan Partnership for New Education, a nonprofit organization that had been involved in other education reform activities, emerged as the primary statewide assistance provider for charter schools. Working under contract with the Michigan Department of Education, the partnership set out to provide help for charter schools on everything from curriculum design to legal work to accounting.[21] The partnership also raised money privately to establish a loan pool to help charter schools meet cash-flow needs while they waited for state funds; the pool lent $1.8 million to 18 schools.

Though the partnership has since dissolved, other organizations have stepped into the breach. One is the Michigan Association of Public School Academies, a trade association that provides technical assistance and access to shared services for charter schools across Michigan. Another is Central Michigan University's Resource Center for Charter Schools, which offers services in three main areas: assessment, evaluation, and validation; curriculum and technology services; and business, management, and operational services.[22]

In Colorado, the Gates Foundation provided seed money for the Colorado League of Charter Schools, which helped groups prepare applications, provided legal advice and assisted schools in negotiations with school districts (especially critical in Colorado), developed model policies that schools can modify as needed, conducted statewide public relations and media work for charter schools, advocated for charter schools' interests in the state legislature, and held meetings and conferences where charter schools could exchange ideas and gain access to experts.[23] Colorado charter schools also received substantial assistance from their state department of education, whose one-person charter school unit published regular newsletters filled with useful information and provided one-on-one assistance to schools as needed.[24]

In Massachusetts the Pioneer Institute, a conservative, business-funded think tank that played a role in passing charter school legislation, established the Charter School Resource Center to help new schools succeed. The Resource Center published the *Charter School Handbook*, which provides guidance for schools on the whole range of charter school issues. The center also regularly convened charter school officials during the early months of the program to share ideas, and its staff conducted "audits" of the schools to help prepare them for any later real audits. More generally, the Resource Center acted as the "yellow pages" for charter schools, connecting them with outside resources as needed.[25]

Fifth, some charter schools contracted with existing school districts as a way to hold down costs. In Georgia, of course, the schools were so integrated with their districts that this sort of cooperation was the norm, and "contracting" is not the right word to describe the relationship. Charter schools were just part of districts' administrative systems and thus had access to the scale economies districts enjoy. In Colorado, although charter schools were administratively part of school districts, they had to work out the details of their relationships case by case. Some schools worked out mutually beneficial arrangements with their districts on such services as transporting students to charter schools and providing special education. Others were unable to do so because relations with districts were too tense. Tension was more the norm in Massachusetts and Michigan, where schools reported very little administrative involvement with their local school districts. The one exception in Michigan was that some charter schools struck up positive working relationships with "intermediate school districts" (ISDs), regional agencies that provide some services to school districts. Even some schools that received their charters from universities were able to contract with ISDs for services, most commonly special education.

Discussion and Conclusion

From this survey of charter school finances in four states with very different charter laws, the importance of legislative compromise to the financial fortunes of the schools is apparent in at least three ways. First, laws that restrict the ability of public or private schools to convert to charter status worsen the overall financial health of the charter school sector. Both the Michigan data and interviews with charter officials make clear that start-from-scratch schools have a more difficult time financially. By requiring that charter schools be brand-new schools, policymakers create a bleaker financial picture for charter schools on average.

Second, the residual regulatory burden affects charter schools' finances negatively as well. The previous chapter argued that this residual burden had little impact on charter schools' ability to conduct their core activities according to their own plans. But these regulations had the effect of raising charter schools' costs in two ways: by imposing the sheer cost of compliance, which charter schools had to meet without the economies of scale enjoyed by conventional districts; and by restricting the ability of charter schools to act creatively to reduce costs. Primary examples of compliance costs included reporting and record-keeping and special education. Restricting schools' efforts to creatively reduce costs was exemplified by one school's inability to institute an innovative, lower-cost lunch arrangement. Though most residual laws and regulations did not steer charter schools in unwanted educational directions, they did induce the schools to divert resources from other activities.

Third, limits on the amount of funds charter schools could receive had a negative financial impact. In all the states (except Georgia, where all charter schools by law already had a facility), the inaccessibility of capital funding exacerbated one of charter schools' most vexing financial challenges: acquiring and renovating facilities. Even for ongoing expenses, both the Michigan data and interviews suggest that regular state revenues were often not enough for charter schools to make ends meet. Legislation had the potential to make this situation worse by limiting the schools' per-pupil funding to something below average costs, as happened in Colorado.

Compromises such as these made it more difficult for charter school programs to accomplish their purposes. But two additional issues confound this straightforward story of compromise tripping up implementation. First, most of the schools' financial difficulties arose not from legislative compromise but from legislative *success* in guaranteeing charter schools independence and autonomy from local school districts. It is the schools' independence that created the need to incur such massive startup expenses; independence that sent charter schools on the challenging quest for facilities; independence that cut charter schools off from the economies of scale to which regular schools have access; independence that made it difficult in many cases for charter schools to contract back with school districts for services. Certainly, independence is vital if charter schools are to serve their educational purposes. No charter school interviewed in Colorado, Massachusetts, or Michigan would have traded its autonomy for the financial security enjoyed by Georgia's schools. The point here is just that independence is a double-edged sword that creates problems for charter schools even as it creates opportunities.

Second, the experience in these four states suggests that though legislative decisions set important financial boundaries, they do not determine how charter schools will fare financially. Even though legislative compromises raised charter schools' costs and limited their revenues, no charter schools in these states went out of business because of financial insolvency or for any other reason during the period covered by this study. Charter schools have managed to make ends meet by raising public and private grants, mobilizing volunteer efforts, joining forces with trade associations and resource centers, and in some cases, contracting with school districts for services. In many ways, the most compelling financial story is what charter schools were able to do despite the constraints they faced.

6 | *Challenging the System*

"**D**ESPITE WHAT the words seem to imply, 'charter schools' is not basically about the schools." So writes Ted Kolderie, one of the progenitors of the charter idea. He continues: "For the teachers who found them and the students who enroll in them, true, it is the schools that are important. But for others, from the beginning, 'charter schools' has been about system-reform . . . a way for the state to cause the district system to improve."[1]

In theory, charter schools might help change the existing system through three mechanisms. First, as *laboratories* free from law and regulation, charter schools experiment with new educational practices that might be replicated on a broader scale in many public schools.[2] Second, as *competitors* to school districts, charter schools take money from public schools for each child they enroll. Districts have a financial incentive to persuade families not to leave the public school system. Districts might have other reasons to compete vigorously with charter schools, such as retaining star teachers or maintaining the district's reputation in the community. Consequently, it is argued, districts will respond to the presence (or even the potential presence) of charter schools by improving their offerings. Third, charter schools might, over time, simply *replace* district schools as purveyors of public education. As more and more families choose charter schools, conventional district schools will serve a smaller and smaller fraction of the public school population.

These three theses differ from one another primarily in their assessments of conventional school districts' ability to change for the better. The laboratory thesis is the most optimistic, positing that the mere demonstration that some idea or another "works" will persuade many school districts to adopt the innovation. The replacement thesis is the least optimistic, predicting that conventional districts will muddle along in their familiar fashion until they fade into oblivion. The competition thesis lies in between, hypothesizing that conventional districts can change for the better, but only with the introduction of a quasi-market for public education.

To be sure, charter schools could still serve a useful educational function even if they did not effect these system changes. For example, charter schools could effectively serve the needs of groups of students who have not been well served in conventional schools, such as children with certain types of special needs, students with unique learning styles, or young people who have dropped out of school or run afoul of the law.[3] Charter schools could achieve, in effect, a limited version of the replacement mechanism described above—replacing district schools in a restricted part of the student market. Arguably, if charter schools served this purpose but had no further impact on American education, one could deem the charter school experiment a success. But the claims of charter advocates extend beyond this limited impact. To assess whether charter schools can fulfill their *full* promise, it is important to examine the three mechanisms of system change as well.

For any of these three mechanisms to operate, charter schools need sufficient autonomy to differentiate themselves and the financial wherewithal to make ends meet, the subjects that preceding chapters addressed. But differentiation and viability are only *necessary* conditions for impact. These are conditions that, in Kolderie's words, are "about the schools." For a charter school program to have an impact on existing school districts, autonomy and viability of particular schools must leverage broader change.

Unlike other issues discussed in this study, the broader impact of charter schools does not lend itself as easily to empirical examination of the links between legislation and outcome. As with many complex educational reforms, the dynamics of district response to charter schools are likely to entail a long-term process, the results of which may not yet be apparent. But because the issue of impact is so vital, a full examination of charter school programs must glean whatever empirical hints there are from the existing record. This chapter examines each of the three mechanisms for impact in turn. In general, I am pessimistic about the potential of many charter school programs as they are now constituted to have the broader impact their proponents intend. Among the obstacles are the legislative compromises that have been struck in the process of passing charter school laws. I am also concerned about the assumptions underlying the hypothesized mechanisms of impact.

Research on questions of system impact is only beginning to emerge. Eric Rofes's 1998 study of 25 school districts provides extensive interview data about the impact charter schools have had on districts and districts' responses.[4] Robert Maranto and his associates have completed a quantitative analysis of survey data regarding changes perceived by Arizona school teachers in the wake of charter reform in that state.[5] The analysis that follows draws on my own research as well as those two studies.

The Laboratory Thesis

As discussed in previous chapters, legislative compromises have undermined the autonomy enjoyed by charter schools in many states. In Georgia these compromises were so severe that charter schools have virtually no more latitude than conventional public schools enjoy on the core elements of school decisionmaking. Without latitude, the idea that charter schools will serve as the "R&D department" for public education seems absurd. But in many states, including the three others examined in this book (Colorado, Massachusetts, and Michigan), the foregoing analysis suggests that in most important areas of school decisionmaking charter schools have wide latitude to chart their own course. Since charter schools in these states have the authority to innovate, perhaps the prospects for the laboratory thesis are brighter there.

The idea that charter schools will serve as R&D departments for public education, though, appears doubtful in these states as well because of two questionable assumptions underlying the laboratory thesis. The first is that charter schools will use their latitude to engage in activities to which school districts would have had no exposure, giving districts the chance to adopt practices that otherwise would have been unknown to them. But charter schools in Colorado, Massachusetts, and Michigan have generally not engaged in activities that conventional districts would regard as new and path-breaking. To be sure, charter schools have done interesting and varied things with their curricula, their instructional practices, their staffing, their budgets, and their governance. But the innovations that charter schools have undertaken are, by and large, innovations that have been proposed elsewhere and, to a limited extent, carried out by existing public schools.[6] Of the 80 schools whose profiles form the basis for Table 4-3, some 54 percent are pursuing a "basics" approach, a standard vocational education model, a subject-focused curriculum (like arts or science and math), or a general or not-identifiable educational approach. Nine percent are following culture-centric models, which though unusual have certainly been well publicized in the national education press and literature. The remaining 36 percent indeed list alternative educational approaches. But many of these, though "alternative," are based on widely known models such as Montessori. As a result, it seems unlikely that many school districts would adopt the practices of charter schools solely on their merits. Most school districts have already been exposed to the ideas charter schools are implementing and have chosen not to adopt them.[7]

I offer two qualifications to this conclusion, however. First, although the individual practices of most charter schools may not be radically innovative, there is evidence that charter schools link their practices together in comprehensive "innovation systems" to focus on a coherent mission. One study of innovation in Massachusetts charter schools found that the commitment of charter staffs and their broader constituencies to their schools' missions created a strong sense of community at the schools. Innovative practices were common in district schools as well, but they were generally added on to existing programs rather than part of comprehensive overhauls of school operations.[8] If charter schools are to serve as a model for conventional public schools, what they appear to be demonstrating is the importance of a coherent focus rather than the value of any particular classroom or management practices.

Second, although individual school practices may only rarely serve as models for conventional schools, the broader institutional regime through which charter schools come to be and in which they are regulated is itself a genuine innovation. The unique character of charter schools is their institutional setting: new or converted schools are formed by self-organized teams of people, who are then granted substantial authority to deploy their designs. They set a mission that can be more targeted and specific than that of a conventional public school, which must strive to be all things to all people. They deploy their designs in an environment that allows broad latitude within the constraints of the marketplace and the contracts the schools sign promising certain levels of performance. It is this constellation of institutional arrangements that makes charter schools truly unique.

If charter schools are to serve as laboratories, then, they are most likely to do so as examples of an institutional form rather than as innovators in curriculum or assessment or some other aspect of practice. Pioneering school districts, for example, might decide they like the idea of asking prospective school operators to submit competitive proposals to run schools, rather than just granting that authority automatically to the staff already in place within a school. They might adopt the notion of requiring each school to sign a charter or contract, specifying the school's obligations over a period of time. Districts might be persuaded to grant schools the real authority many charter schools have, taking a step beyond the typically thin forms of "school-based management" present in many jurisdictions today. In taking these steps, districts could learn from the early experiences of charter school programs. Charter schools would serve as laboratories, not so much for the classroom and management practices they adopt but for the broader set of arrangements under which they work.[9]

A second questionable assumption underlying the laboratory thesis is that new ideas will diffuse once shown to be successful. Richard F. Elmore argues convincingly that even highly organized and well-funded efforts to replicate "good ideas" in American education have foundered, largely because existing institutions and personnel lack incentives to adopt new ideas, no matter how "good." Elmore chronicles the history of many such efforts and their limited impact on practice.[10]

A case in point is the New American Schools project, which has funded several teams to develop whole-school designs and then work with schools and districts to implement them.[11] This strategy shares some kinship with the charter idea, focusing as it does on designing entire schools on paper, trying the ideas out in a few schools, and then implementing the designs widely. Though many observers are enthusiastic about the designs that have emerged and several school districts (and some entire states) are working with New American Schools to implement them, their efforts have shown how daunting the task is. Efforts to implement the designs have fallen victim to everything from lack of local capacity to political infighting.[12]

If a project like New American Schools has difficulty diffusing good ideas on their merits, it is difficult to imagine charter schools' ideas spreading widely purely on the basis of their success. New American Schools is a deliberate effort to diffuse whole-school innovations, complete with a national staff and a multi-million-dollar annual budget. Charter schools, by contrast, tend to be independent organizations whose leaders may or may not be interested in diffusion. Even those who are committed to diffusion have limited time to devote to spreading the word about what they are doing, much less provide existing public schools with the hands-on technical assistance New American Schools offers.[13]

In short, charter schools are unlikely to transform public education by serving as laboratories for "good ideas" at the school level. In some states, the schools' potential to experiment has been undermined by legislative compromise. But the laboratory mechanism also seems unlikely to work because the assumptions that underlie it are questionable. There is little evidence that charter schools are using their latitude to engage in completely "new" activities, and still less that even highly successful, highly experimental ideas diffuse readily in American education. For the laboratory mechanism to function, something more basic would have to change in the governance of public education. Such shifts in governance, in the incentives facing the operators of schools, are precisely what the other two mechanisms for impact invoke.

The Competition Thesis

Can charter schools have a broad impact on American education by competing with districts for students, and thus for funding? As is the case with the laboratory thesis, the mechanism of competition appears hampered by legislative compromises, and more careful thinking about how competition might work in practice raises some additional challenges to the thesis.

Legislative compromise might undermine competition in one of three ways. First, legislators could limit the number of charter schools in a state or district, statutorily capping scale, and by consequence, response and impact. Second, legislation could cushion the financial blow to existing districts when students choose charter schools, lessening the incentive to respond. Finally, legislative issues discussed in previous chapters could have implications for impact as well. Even if legislation imposes no numerical limits on charter schools, it can institute de facto caps by making the "business" of running a charter school less viable or by placing decisionmaking authority over charter schools in the hands of school districts.

At the time of this study, three of the four states had placed a cap on the number of charter schools that could be open at any one time. The Massachusetts law was the most severe, limiting the number of schools to 25 and the proportion of the state's students who could attend to three-quarters of 1 percent. Colorado placed a cap of 50. Michigan's law set a gradually increasing cap, authorizing up to 85 schools in 1996 and as many as 150 in 1999. But Massachusetts had nearly 1,800 public schools in 1993; Colorado more than 1,400 and Michigan almost 3,500.[14] Of the four states, only Georgia allowed an unlimited number of charter schools to open.

All four states also cushioned the financial impact on school districts in some respect. In Massachusetts, the original charter bill called for funding to follow the child from regular public districts to charter schools.

But subsequent legislation appropriated funds to reimburse many districts at least partially for the losses they incurred when students chose charter schools.[15] In theory, these reimbursements were temporary, but will legislators resist pressure to extend them? In Georgia, funding did not follow the child in any meaningful respect. Charter schools remained fiscally part of the school district, and in any case they were only conversions of public schools. It would not be a stretch to say that charter schools imposed no fiscal consequences on districts. In Colorado, initial legislation sought to limit the fiscal impact on districts by requiring charter schools to negotiate funding with districts, perhaps receiving as little as 80 percent of per-pupil operating revenues, or 52 percent of actual per-pupil costs. Since districts presumably realize some cost savings when children leave, though, this amount still may represent minimal *net* fiscal impact to most districts. Michigan was the only state in this study where districts felt nearly the full financial effect of students' choices. Even there, charter schools were not entitled to a share of district funds for capital expenditures.

Finally, legislatures have also struck compromises on the viability and autonomy of schools that have implications for their ability to serve as competitors. Even without caps on numbers, the potential for scale in these states is limited by issues of institutional viability (see Chapter 5). No charter school law provided charter schools with facilities or with ample startup funds, leaving the schools to raise the resources they needed through donations of money and expertise. The first crop of charter schools largely succeeded in this regard, but would hundreds of charter schools be able to do the same? Philanthropic resources and volunteer efforts that are available to a few high-profile schools might not expand to cover a larger "sector" of charter schools. Second, the granting of exclusive chartering authority to local school boards in Georgia neutralized that state's provision for an unlimited number of charters. With local boards in full control, only three charter schools had opened by the 1995–96 school year.

Even without these compromises, though, there are reasons to believe the competition mechanism might not always work as the proponents of charter schools expect. The assumption that underlies the competition theory is that school districts will respond to competition in a particular way: that is, by improving the quality of the education they offer to students. Evidence from the four states, however, suggests that districts have a whole array of possible responses to the introduction of competition. Many of these have little to do with improving the quality of public education; some, perversely, are likely to have the opposite effect. Here are five prominent examples from the four states in this study.

1. *Use the courts to derail or restrict charter schools.* In the three states with strong laws, districts and/or other opponents of charter schools have filed lawsuits challenging the charter law or specific applications of it. The most successful case was a lawsuit filed in Michigan by a range of individuals and organizations, including the Council About Parochiaid (a broad coalition of education interest groups), three members of the state board of education, a member of a local board of education, the Michigan Education Association, and the Michigan chapter of the American Civil Liberties Union. The plaintiffs argued that the law violated the state constitution's ban on spending public money on private schools and that it usurped the state board of education's rightful authority over public education. In October 1994, an Ingham County Circuit Court judge enjoined the state from releasing state funds to the ten charter schools then open; he struck down the law the next month. In response, the legislature rewrote the charter law to make clear the state board of education's ultimate authority over charter schools, their public nature, and the constraints they faced as public schools.[16]

2. *Use subsequent legislation to derail or restrict charter schools.* Districts and other opponents of charter schools, rather than competing constructively, can also attempt to persuade the legislature to scale back the charter program or minimize its impact on existing schools. Massachusetts represents the most striking example of this phenomenon. As noted above, Massachusetts districts persuaded legislators to reimburse many of them, at least partially and temporarily, for funds they lost to charter schools. In Michigan as well, districts and their allies have prompted legislators to weaken the law in important respects. The 1995 school code revisions in that state, for example, made charter schools subject to virtually all public school law. In an attempt to restrict the chartering activity of prolific Central Michigan University, the new law

also prohibited any one sponsor from chartering more than half of the state's charter schools: 42 in 1996, 75 in 1999.[17]

3. *Use other means to make life difficult for charter schools.* Districts and other charter opponents have also used other tactics to undermine individual charter schools.[18] As Tom Loveless and Claudia Jasin write: "In this study [of eight new charter schools in Massachusetts], state political battles were fought all over again in several towns, this time with players wielding different degrees of power. School committees, district superintendents, and local newspapers—defeated in the legislative debate—loom powerfully in the local politics of Massachusetts' charter schools."[19] These tactics included:

—alleged harassment of charter school organizers and prospective students and parents;[20]
—refusal to provide student records to a charter school until well after school started, complicating the schools' efforts to divide students into classes, choose appropriate materials, and devise plans for special education students;[21]
—one school system's efforts to persuade a congregation to lease space to it instead of the local charter school, which had been housed in a motel.[22]

Some responses along these lines came not from school districts per se but from other opponents of charter schools. A local office of the Michigan Education Association raised a stir by writing a letter to a university president threatening various actions if the university chartered schools that did not meet the MEA's standards. These standards included close cooperation with the local school district and adherence to all provisions of relevant collective bargaining agreements. If the university chartered schools that fell outside these guidelines, the letter said, union members would not accept university students as student teachers, would not donate money to the university, and would not participate in university graduate or training programs.[23] In another incident, a school district seeking to sell a vacant school building placed a restriction in the deed preventing its use as a school—a provision apparently aimed at blocking a local charter school from using the facility.[24]

4. *Respond to fiscal stress not by improving but by threatening to cut back*

on popular programs. One school district in Massachusetts announced that because of a charter school the district would have to eliminate art and advanced-placement courses, reduce the number of sports programs, close after-school services, and end tutoring programs.[25] In Colorado, Jefferson County's school board president told the *Denver Post*: "For every charter school I approve I may have to tell someone that this will cut their student's sports program or bus ride, or renegotiate teacher salaries. To give to one place you have to take from another."[26] In 1995, the Denver Public Schools proposed budget cuts that would have eliminated numerous popular programs. In part in response to charter schools' costs, officials said, marching bands, sports, libraries, and enrichment activities would get the ax, and class sizes would rise.[27]

5. *Ignore or peacefully coexist with charter schools.* All of the above responses typify the expected reaction of a monopoly supplier to the presence of competition. But in his famous discussion of monopoly, Albert Hirschman makes a provocative suggestion that is relevant here:

> But there are many other cases where competition does not restrain monopoly as it is supposed to, but *comforts and bolsters* it by unburdening it of some of its more troublesome customers. . . . If, as is likely, the mobile customers are most sensitive to quality, their exit, caused by the poor performance of the local monopolist, permits him to persist in his comfortable mediocrity. . . . Those who hold power in the lazy monopoly may actually have an interest in *creating* some limited opportunities for exit on the part of those whose voice might be uncomfortable.[28]

According to this analysis, as long as charter schools remain a relatively small force, they may prove useful to school districts as "pressure valves." Instead of taking up time at school board meetings, harassing teachers and administrators, and making disparaging remarks about the district in the media, disgruntled parents and voters can occupy themselves with starting a charter school.

School districts may also regard charter schools as places to unload students they regard as undesirable. Certain students impose high financial costs on school districts because they have disabilities or require intensive assistance of other kinds. Others drag down average district test scores. If charter schools are willing to serve high-cost and/or low-performing students, districts might regard their presence as a blessing rather than a curse.[29]

Districts may gain other benefits from charter schools as well. Officials in Douglas County, Colorado, for example, expected annual enrollment growth of 10 percent (2,000–3,000 students per year) through the year 2000, which would require massive capital expansion. In that context, the district did not mind having 500 to 1,000 students enrolled in charter schools, which are responsible for finding their own facilities.[30]

Even if a charter school stimulates a response from its local school district, that response may not be aimed at improving education for the district's young people. In fact, any of the five tactics might have the *opposite* effect. The first four threaten to divert resources from potentially quality-enhancing activities. The fifth, to the extent that districts' most vocal critics exit, reduces rather than increases pressure on districts to change for the better.

Some researchers have begun to collect more systematic evidence on the competitive impact of charter schools. Rofes's study of 25 districts found that "typically, school districts had not responded with swift, dramatic improvements," though about one in four districts had "responded energetically to the advent of charters." Not all districts where enrollment was reduced as a result of the founding of charter schools, however, responded with positive changes. Other factors, such as past performance of the districts and the eagerness of district leadership to undertake change, determined whether districts responded to charter schools by undertaking educational reforms.[31] Maranto and his associates' surveys of teachers found significantly more school-level innovation in Arizona, with its strong charter law, than in Nevada, with its weak law. This research also found that schools in Arizona that were strongly affected by charters were more likely than less-affected schools to adopt higher-cost reforms.[32]

In addition, many anecdotes suggest that districts respond to the presence (or anticipated presence) of charter schools by improving their educational offerings. Boston, for example, has created "pilot schools," charter-like schools that operate within the Boston system but are free of many of the constraints imposed by district policy or collective-bargaining agreements. Because the school system established pilot schools shortly after the passage of charter legislation, its action has been widely cited by charter advocates as an example of the ripple effects charter schools can produce.[33] Similarly, Boulder Valley School District in Colorado established "focus schools," quasi-independent schools with a charter-like application process.[34] Also in Colorado, parents in Jefferson County, the state's largest school district, had long clamored for the expansion or replication of an oversubscribed alternative school established by the district many years earlier. Despite a waiting list of 1,000 students and numerous calls for expansion, including one by an internal committee of the district, the school board refused. After the charter law passed and parents began organizing a charter school, however, the district agreed to establish a new alternative program, governed in part by those organizing the charter school. By spring 1994, the district had more than doubled the number of alternative schools: some charter, some district-run.[35] The charter school literature contains many other such anecdotes,[36] but anecdotes about nonconstructive responses are just as prevalent.

One possible explanation for districts' nonconstructive responses, of course, is that the legislative compromises that limit competition have made these other strategies possible. Only because the potential for competition is so minimal have districts chosen to respond to charter schools in ways that do nothing to improve—and may in fact degrade—the quality of education they offer. This response certainly applies to the fifth example: Hirschman's lazy monopolist wants "limited opportunities for exit," not the possibility of mass exodus. The "Washington Monument" response, too, assumes a limited loss of funds to charter schools. Faced with a massive loss of funds, one could argue, school districts could no longer afford to play public relations games with popular programs. But the first three responses—using the courts, the legislature, and nuisance tactics—seem likely only to intensify as competition grows. Even a district with many potential charter schools might find these responses more cost-effective than a wholesale revamping of its practices.

Even in the face of significant competition, reworking an entire school district for high performance is very difficult. The tasks of devising and implementing wide-ranging reforms are extremely complex and daunting. This is true even for organizations in highly competitive markets, as recent studies of corporate efforts to "reengineer" their operations have shown.[37] Wholesale change is also difficult because of political phenomena of exactly the sort this study has described at the state level. Those with an interest in the status quo are likely to resist change even in the face of a loss in a district's competitive position. If wide-scale reform were easy to effect, surely it would already be more common in light of the wide criticism of public schools and political pressure for significant improvement. Competition from charter schools may not be substantial enough to change the basic calculation most districts appear to have made.

The Replacement Thesis

For those who believe districts are unlikely to respond constructively to the presence of charter schools, the replacement thesis stands as the last hope of systemic impact. Perhaps charter schools will transform public education by gradually withdrawing students and funds from conventional districts until charter schools are the primary vehicle for the delivery of public education. Until now, of course, the legislative compromises described in the previous section have made the replacement hypothesis seem unrealistic. Nowhere in the country are charter schools approaching a scale where one would regard them as replacing public schools. Exceptions are most likely to emerge in school districts with very low enrollment, such as rural districts. In these areas, a good-sized charter school could indeed overtake the district as the leading provider of public education. In larger systems, where most students reside, many more charter schools would have to open for replacement to occur.

Like the other two mechanisms, though, the replacement mechanism might have trouble working even if the charter idea were enacted fully and without compromise by a state legislature. Replacement would require a massive increase in the independent supply of public education. The United States has some 88,000 public schools. Even if charter schools were the same size as the regular public schools they replaced, more than 40,000 would need to be created (or converted) just to replace half of the conventional public system.

Given the extraordinary demands of starting a new school from scratch, the conversion of existing public or private schools would likely have to play a major role in this expansion. Otherwise, the "charterization" of public schools would be akin to deregulating local telephone service by allowing dozens of companies to lay separate fiber-optic networks throughout a city rather than arranging for competitors to tap into the existing monopolist's infrastructure. It also seems unlikely that such a massive ramp-up would be accomplished by 80,000 groups of dedicated individuals sitting around their kitchen tables dreaming up new school designs. More plausible is the scenario under which a handful of large organizations—whether for-profit outfits like the Edison Project or non-profit efforts like New American Schools—each sponsors a large number of charter schools nationwide.

A charter school movement large enough to begin replacing district schools, then, would probably need to rely heavily on converted schools and "franchise" operations of large education service organizations. Whether such developments would be positive or negative is beyond the scope of this study. But it seems clear that the resulting charter school sector would look very little like today's fledgling band of charter schools.

Conclusion

As they are now constituted, many states' charter school programs will have difficulty achieving the system-changing impact their proponents envision. In part, they are limited by legislative compromises that diminish charter schools' ability to act as effective laboratories, competitors, or replacements for existing district schools. Most notable among these are restrictions on the number of charter schools that can open.

But the systemic impact of charter schools may also be limited by problems with the assumptions that underlie the three mechanisms of impact explored in this chapter. As laboratories, charter schools appear unlikely to provide models of classroom practice that are replicated on a broad scale. Existing charter schools have not engaged in many truly "new" educational practices, and districts are unlikely to adopt curricular innovations that work. (More likely, perhaps, is that the broader institutional regime that agencies are developing for charter schools might serve as a model for the governance of public education more generally.) As competitors, charter schools appear capable of stimulating a response. But since a constructive response (vast improvement in educational offerings) is so difficult to effect, districts often turn to other ways of dealing with competition, some of which may actually detract from the quality of education. As a replacement for the existing system, the charter sector would have to undergo an expansion so massive that it would almost certainly transform not just the scale but the very character of the charter school movement.

Fulfilling the Promise of Charter Schools

III

7 | Politics, Policy, and the Future of Charter School Programs

THE GROWTH of the charter school movement in the 1990s was nothing less than phenomenal. From a single state law in 1991, by 1998 charter school legislation had proliferated to two-thirds of the states. More than a thousand schools, most of them brand new, educating hundreds of thousands of students, have followed. But will this early momentum propel the charter school movement into a future of real impact? The evidence suggests that momentum alone will not be enough. For charter schools to realize their full promise, the charter school landscape will have to change in three ways. First, charter school laws will have to be strengthened if charter schools are going to have a lasting impact on public education. Second, a more substantial infrastructure of support will need to be developed to make charter schools sustainable as a large-scale reform. Third, agencies that oversee charter schools will need to develop new paradigms of oversight that make sense in a world of independent public schools.

Policy *laws*

Charter school laws vary greatly from state to state, and these variations have significant consequences for the potential success of charter

147

school policies. Compromises in state legislatures have constrained the autonomy of charter schools, their viability as organizations, and their potential to have an impact on public education as a whole. Because of these compromises, only a few states have truly engaged in an experiment with charter schools. In most states with charter laws, the statutes are too far removed from "ideal" charter legislation for anyone to say whether charter schools are working or not.

If states want to give charter schools a full test, legislatures will need to consider passing new laws or changing existing laws to include specific provisions that are central to the charter school idea. The list of such provisions is potentially a long one, but four would appear to be most important:

1. *The authority for a nonlocal body to approve charter schools.* Many state charter school laws grant local school boards a great deal of say over the creation of charter schools in their jurisdictions. In fact, at the end of 1998 only 21 of the 35 charter school laws empowered any entity to grant charters without the agreement of the local board (see Table 7-1).[1] The other 14 gave local boards veto power over the opening of charter schools in their areas. As Chapter 4 indicated, districts have used this authority to restrict the proliferation of charter schools and to limit their potential for impact on conventional public schools. Georgia's placement of veto power in the hands of local school boards has led to a relatively slow spread of charter schools in the state and to a set of charter schools that departs only minimally from existing practice. Colorado's system, while not placing the final say in the hands of local boards, has still given districts the opportunity to restrict the growth of the charter sector and to block the creation of charter schools with the potential to have a large fiscal impact.

If states want to give charter schools the autonomy to break the mold and the opportunity to challenge existing districts in the marketplace, legislatures need to empower nonlocal entities to approve charter schools. Existing laws grant this authority to a range of bodies, including state boards of education, boards of public universities and community colleges, boards of regional service agencies for public school districts, stand-alone charter school boards or committees, and city councils. To be sure, legislatures need to consider the capacity of such entities to make diffi-

Table 7-1. *Key Provisions of Charter Laws in 34 States and the District of Columbia*

State	No veto possible by local school board	Legal independence possible	Full per-pupil operating funds follow children	Minimal restrictions on source and number of schools	Number of provisions included
Alaska					0
Arizona	•	•	•	•	4
Arkansas					0
California	•	•	•	•	4
Colorado	•	•		•	3
Connecticut	•	•	•		3
Delaware	•	•	•		3
District of Columbia	•	•	•	•	4
Florida		•		•	2
Georgia				•	1
Hawaii			•		1
Idaho					0
Illinois	•	•	•		3
Kansas					0
Louisiana			•		1
Massachusetts	•	•			2
Michigan	•	•	•	•	4
Minnesota	•	•	•	•	4
Mississippi					0
Missouri	•	•	•	•	4
Nevada			•		1
New Hampshire		•		•	2
New Jersey	•	•		•	3
New Mexico	•				1
New York	•	•	•	•	4
North Carolina	•	•	•	•	4
Ohio	•	•	•		3
Pennsylvania	a	•		•	2
Rhode Island	•		•		2
South Carolina	•		•	•	3
Texas	•	•	•	•	4
Utah	•				1
Virginia					0
Wisconsin	b	•		•	2
Wyoming	•			•	2
Number of laws with provision	21 of 35	20 of 35	18 of 35	18 of 35	...

a. Beginning in 1999–2000, the Pennsylvania state board of education may grant charters upon appeal to applicants denied locally.

b. Amendments to Wisconsin's law in 1997 created alternative charter authorizers, but only in the city of Milwaukee. Because of the limited geographic area covered by this provision, this table still codes Wisconsin's law as allowing local veto.

cult decisions about whether to grant charters and to conduct the monitoring and evaluation required to hold charter schools accountable for results. Some agencies will be better suited for these roles than others. But state legislatures interested in creating charter school programs that afford real autonomy and real potential for impact should survey their states' terrain and identify the most promising candidates to serve these functions. If they do not, charter school programs will not have the chance to live up to their full potential.

2. *Legal independence of charter schools.* Only 20 of the 35 charter laws on the books at the end of 1998 allowed charter schools to exist as separate legal entities. In the other 15 states, charter schools had no independent legal status; like conventional public schools, they were to be treated as divisions of their local school districts. And some of the 20 states that allowed legal independence did not require it. In California's initial charter law, for example, a charter school's legal status was determined by the charter agreement hammered out between the school and the district.[2]

The experience in Colorado, chronicled in Chapter 4, suggests that it is possible for charter schools to operate autonomously without formal independence. In Colorado, charter schools were units of local school districts with no independent legal status, and yet they appear to have operated with relative freedom from constraint on the core elements of schooling. But in Colorado, the state board of education has indicated a willingness to overturn local school board decisions regarding charter schools, including decisions about the terms under which charters and districts relate to each other. Because of the state board's oversight, districts have had to grant charters effective independence even in the absence of legal independence. In other states (or in Colorado under different political circumstances) charter schools might not find themselves in the same position. In Georgia, for example, charter schools reported having no more latitude than other public schools in their districts.

To ensure that charter schools have the autonomy to innovate and to act independently of their school districts, state legislatures should establish charter schools as distinct legal entities. In many states, charter schools exist as nonprofit corporations, a status that provides the schools with clear legal standing. Each state, however, needs to consider the complexities of its own situation. In some states, for example, nonprofit status may compromise charter schools' ability to enroll their employees in state retirement systems. In such cases, states have established charter schools as "public authorities" of one kind or another. Whatever precise form they take, these provisions form an essential foundation for charter schools' autonomy.

Another aspect of charter schools' independence is the scope of exemptions they receive from state law and regulation. In the charter school ideal, schools receive broad automatic exemptions from most state law, with the exception of provisions regarding health, safety, nondiscrimination, nonreligiosity, and a handful of other core public school laws. The research reported in Chapter 4, however, suggests that this aspect of charter school law is less important than legal independence and the availability of nonlocal authorizers. In Michigan, for example, charter schools have virtually no exemptions from state law and regulation. Yet they enjoy substantial independence because of their legal status and the fact that most were authorized by bodies other than conventional school districts. Most of the state laws they are required to follow operate at the periphery of schooling—the reports they are required to file, for instance—and not at the core. This is not to say that broad automatic exemptions are not a worthy target for charter school advocates. Rather, the point is simply that legal independence and nonlocal authorizers should come first on a short list of critical provisions.

3. *Full per-pupil funding that follows children to charter schools.* Full per-pupil funding is important for two reasons. First, it is essential to the financial viability of charter schools themselves. Chapter 5 documented the financial challenges of starting and operating an independent public school; without a fair share of per-pupil funding, charter schools cannot hope to innovate or compete in public education. Second, full per-pupil funding is the primary mechanism through which charter schools can have an impact on regular public schools. Only if funding follows children from districts to charter schools will charter schools create significant incentives for districts to improve.

And yet only 18 of the 35 states with charter laws at the end of 1998 mandated that full per-pupil operating dollars follow children to charter schools. The other 17 laws fell into one of three categories: (1) laws that explicitly allowed charter schools to receive less than 100 percent of per-pupil operating dollars; (2) laws that provided full funding to charter schools but did not take any money away from districts for the students who left for charter schools (i.e., money did not follow children); or (3) laws that were silent on the amount of funding charter schools could receive, leaving the determination to local school districts. Even in most of the 17 states with full per-pupil funding, charter schools received only a share of per-pupil operating dollars. Only a handful of states provided additional money to pay for facilities. As a result, even in states with relatively generous funding, charter schools had to pay for facilities with operating dollars.

To create fertile ground for charter schools that can have an impact, state legislatures should require full per-pupil funding (including money for facilities) to follow children from school districts to charter schools. Only by doing so will they ensure that otherwise successful charter schools are financially viable and that districts have incentives to improve in response to competition from charter schools. Legislatures should also ensure that charter schools have access to fiscal advantages enjoyed by school districts, such as tax-exempt financing and exemptions from property taxes.

4. *Minimal constraints on the source and number of charter schools.* For charter schools to flourish, laws need to allow a wide range of individuals and groups to start charter schools and to allow a large number of charter schools to open. Otherwise, experimentation is stifled and competition restricted. Yet only 18 of the 35 states with laws at the end of 1998 allowed both a wide range of school-initiators and a large number of schools to open. The rest of the states restricted potential charter operators (for example, by requiring charters to be conversions of existing public schools), placed strict caps on the number of charter schools, or both. Either type of provision alone can hamper the effectiveness of charter school programs. Until 1998, Georgia's law allowed an unlimited number of charter schools to open but enabled only existing public schools to convert to charter status. The latter provision resulted in slow proliferation of schools and limited experimentation regardless of the limitless number of schools possible. In Massachusetts, by contrast, the law allowed virtually anyone to propose a charter school. But since the law also limited the number of charter schools statewide to 25 (and the num-

ber in any district to five or fewer), Massachusetts saw limited charter activity through the end of 1997.[3]

State legislatures eager to give charter schools a full test should examine both of these provisions carefully, crafting charter legislation that does not restrict who is invited to submit applications and how many charters can operate statewide and within a district. Without such freedoms, charter legislation looks more like the modest trials of school-based management that many states pursued in the 1980s and 1990s.

Although it is instructive to consider each of these important provisions in turn, it is also important to remember that all of them work together to create an "ideal" charter law in which charter schools are relatively autonomous, adequately funded, and collectively able to have an impact on district schools. Yet in 1998 only about one in four state laws contained all four of the provisions discussed here. Fifteen contained three of the four. In short, a minority of jurisdictions had put into place a charter school program that closely approximates the charter school idea. In most states, a true test of the charter idea must await changes in state law.

What are the prospects for new laws that do contain these provisions, or for changes in existing laws? As charter school programs grow in size and reach, they seem to unleash two opposing political forces. First, fear of an expanded charter sector mobilizes opponents to block strong legislation. Chapters 2 and 3 painted a sobering picture of the politics of charter schools. Since so many powerful interests are challenged by charter schools, passing legislation containing the provisions outlined here has proven difficult across the country. And as charter schools gain momentum, the stakes may seem even higher to their opponents, who are likely to redouble their efforts to block charter laws that authorize nonlocal chartering entities, legal independence, full funding, and an open door for charter organizers.

The opposing force is the political constituency created as charter schools form and grow within a state. Charter schools change from abstractions to real collections of parents, students, teachers, and community supporters. Those involved with charter schools develop a political interest in maintaining or expanding the autonomy and funding charter schools receive. Those who would like to be part of a charter school but cannot because of caps or waiting lists develop a political interest in making laws more open to new charter schools. Before charter schools exist, opponents must only battle an idea. Once charter schools are up and running, they must battle other people with a clear stake in the outcome of the political debate.

How will these two forces balance out in the years to come? As Chapters 2 and 3 suggested, the outcome will vary from state to state based on a host of political factors that range far beyond the politics of charter schools alone. But by looking briefly at more recent legislative experience, we can begin to see some hints of how these debates will pan out. One set of hints comes from states that have passed *new* charter school laws since January 1996 (the stopping point of Chapter 2's analysis). Through the end of 1998, another 14 states and the District of Columbia added new charter laws to the books (see Table 7-1). These laws contained a mixed bag of provisions. Nine of the 15 granted charter schools legal independence. Nine laws also allowed full per-pupil operating funds to follow children to charter schools. Nine allowed charter schools to open without the blessings of their local school boards. Fewer than half allowed a wide range of entities to start charter schools and a large number to open. All in all, about half contained three or more of the four key provisions examined in Table 7-1. Nationally, then, charter school policymaking between 1996 and 1998 did not depart much from pre-1996 experience. State legislatures enacted stronger and weaker laws in about equal numbers.

Another set of hints comes from recent *revisions* to charter school laws. Fourteen states made substantial revisions to their charter laws in 1997 and 1998. With few exceptions, these changes strengthened the charter law provisions outlined in this chapter. Nine states strengthened the financial position of charter schools (see Table 7-2). Eight states opened up the charter school process by raising numerical caps or empowering new groups to start charter schools. Four states empowered new organizations other than local school boards to grant charters. And three states took steps toward granting charter schools more legal independence. With the exception of North Carolina, which required the state board of education to take into account local school boards' objections to pro-

Table 7-2. *Major Changes to Charter Laws, 1997 and 1998*

State	Granted chartering authority to nonlocal bodies	Took steps toward legal independence for charters	Improved charter schools' financial situation	Raised cap on number of schools allowed or opened process to new groups
Arizona			•	
California				
Colorado		•		
District of Columbia				
Florida		•	•	
Georgia				
Louisiana			•	•
Massachusetts				•
Minnesota	•		•	•
New Hampshire			•	
North Carolina	a		•	
Texas				•
Wisconsin				
Wyoming	•			•

a. Though North Carolina's law still empowers the state board of education to approve charter schools over the objections of local school boards, the General Assembly in 1997 required the state board to take into account "local impact statements" filed by local school boards.

posed charter schools, no states weakened their laws on these issues in 1997 and 1998. The legislation passed during these two years, then, suggests that once charter school laws are in place, charter advocates find themselves in a good position to strengthen existing laws. It appears that in introducing new legislation, charter supporters will have to continue on the same difficult road. But they are likely to fare better once charter schools are up and running within a state.

Infrastructure

Charter school laws are one of the most important determinants of the environment within which charter schools carry out their work. Statutes establish who may start charter schools, through what process, and under what terms. Laws set the rights and obligations of charter schools and the resources they will have at their disposal. But charter laws are not the only determinant of charter schools' success. For example, Chapter 5 pointed out that the financial status of charter schools depended not just on funding formulas but also on how charter schools handled their finances. Charter schools in Michigan, Massachusetts, and Colorado thrived despite a difficult fiscal climate by forming an "infrastructure" of support.

In the context of charter schools, "infrastructure" is often regarded as a dirty word. Charter schools are in some ways the quintessential anti-infrastructural reform. Charter entrepreneurs tend to be fiercely independent, eager to break off from existing structures to forge a separate identity. Many of them blame the administrative infrastructure of school districts and state departments of education for many of the problems that plague public education. Independence, not infrastructure, is the watchword in charter circles.

The research reported here, however, suggests that for the charter school movement to be more than a flash in the pan it will need to continue evolving toward a more sophisticated understanding of the importance of infrastructure for the functioning of individual charter schools and of the movement as a whole. Without an adequate infrastructure, individual charter schools will not be able to enjoy autonomy and financial viability over the long term. And the movement as a whole will not achieve the impact on public education hoped for by charter proponents.

Charter school leaders interviewed for this study recalled being shocked by the administrative burdens of starting and operating an autonomous public school. Many charter school founders entered the charter arena because they wanted to put some kind of educational philosophy into action, but they quickly found their time consumed not by curriculum and instructional practice but by the renovation of facilities, the contracting out of numerous services, the management of their states' complicated accounting and reporting systems, the intricacies of providing transportation to far-flung students, and the like. These duties represented the flip side of autonomy: the need to do a great deal of work that, under more traditional arrangements, would have been carried out by school district personnel.

There are many ways to think about the costs associated with each school's need to manage its own affairs. First, by acting alone, charter schools may pay more for goods and services than they would as part of a larger system. To be sure, they may pay less than some large systems do because of bureaucratic inefficiencies in those larger administrative units. But at least in principle, schools acting alone forgo potential cost savings they could achieve through bulk discounts, better negotiating power, and other scale-related economies. Second, charter schools acting alone may miss out on opportunities to build on knowledge and wisdom forged by the experience of others. Acting alone may mean reinventing the wheel; worse yet, it may mean doing things less effectively than one could do them with access to years of experience by counterparts elsewhere. Finally, and perhaps most important, the quality of charter schools' instructional programs may suffer when so much of their leadership's attention is devoted to the administration of the schools rather than the nurturing of teaching and learning. This study's interviewees expressed personal frustration in this regard, but the potential consequences go beyond leaders' own disappointments.

It is important to note that the challenges reported by interviewees are the challenges of schools that managed to open. Excluded from the sample are potential school entrepreneurs who never opened a school, perhaps because of the daunting nature of the startup process. So it is clear that both existing schools and potential schools need support. If the supply of charter schools is to grow to a level at which real impact is possible, potential school operators will need access to support from the very earliest stages of their projects.[4]

To say that charter schools need infrastructure is not to say that they need to rebuild administrative systems like those from which many charter entrepreneurs fled in the first place. Instead, charter schools and their supporters need to create new forms of infrastructure. They need to develop structures that provide vital support for charter schools while respecting their autonomy, structures that are driven by the needs of schools (and ultimately students) rather than by the mandates of a higher bureaucracy, structures in which schools are customers, not subordinates on organizational charts.

As Chapter 5 documented, schools (and prospective schools) are beginning to find ways to meet their needs for support. Several developments are worthy of note:

—*Resource centers.* Most states with significant charter activity are home to one or more "charter school resource centers," nonprofit organizations dedicated to serving the needs of charter schools. Resource centers conduct outreach to prospective charter operators, hold events such as conferences, training sessions, and job fairs, engage in one-on-one consulting with charter school applicants and operators, produce "charter school handbooks," work with the media and policymakers to create a positive climate for charter schools, and serve as brokers between charter schools and resource providers.

—*Associations.* In several states, existing charter schools have formed associations to advocate on their behalf in state legislatures, organize joint purchasing arrangements, help charter schools form a network of support among themselves, and otherwise take advantage of strength in numbers.

—*Vendors.* As charter schools approach becoming a $1 billion industry, vendors of a host of services have naturally taken an interest. These include companies that offer to manage an entire school's operations, from instructional design to custodial services, as well as companies with more specific wares to sell, such as transportation, food service, health insurance, and accounting services.

—*Governmental activity.* In some states, government agencies charged with vetting charter school applications have also sought to provide technical assistance to charter schools. State departments of education, for example, have established "offices of charter schools" that stage workshops for charter applicants, hold training sessions for approved schools, and provide one-on-one consultations.

Many in the charter movement regard the emergent diversity of providers as a positive development that gives schools choices about where to turn for help and keeps providers on their toes. In this early stage of charter school development, there is much more than enough work to keep a host of nonprofits, vendors, and government agencies busy. But as the web of support becomes more dense, each player will need to focus its energies where it can add the most value for charter schools.

New Paradigms of Oversight

For charter schools to be viable, they need support. But they also need to exist in a regulatory climate that holds them accountable without imposing unnecessary burdens. Both of these two points—accountability and minimal burden—are vital to the charter idea. In some respects they are the two sides of the bargain offered by charter schools: accountability in exchange for a grant of autonomy. But designing a system that strikes this balance has proven challenging for charter-granting agencies. It is useful to consider these challenges in two categories: those relating to charter schools' accountability for *academic results*, and those relating to charter schools' accountability for *compliance* with whatever residual regulations apply to charter schools.

Accountability for Academic Results

In principle, each charter school signs a contract with a charter-granting agency that spells out the academic results the school is expected to achieve over the term of its charter. For example, a school might promise that a certain proportion of its students will perform above grade level on a particular assessment or achieve a specific level of improvement over a period of time. When it comes time to consider renewing the school's charter, the charter-granting agency can evaluate the school's progress against these clearly articulated standards. And in cases of extremely low performance, the charter-granting agency could revoke a school's charter before the charter's renewal date.

Behind this simple formulation, though, lies a complex set of issues with which most charter-granting agencies have only just begun to grapple. As a result, the Hudson Institute's nationwide study of charter schools concluded that "today's charter school accountability systems remain underdeveloped, often clumsy and ill-fitting, and are themselves beset by dilemmas."[5] Charter-granting agencies are struggling with how charter schools should fit into existing state and district standards and testing regimes; how to handle accountability for charter schools with unconventional goals, learning processes, or student populations; how precisely to implement the "meet your goals or lose your charter" requirement; what actions to take before a school's renewal date (if any) if a school is not performing adequately; and the basic question: how good is good enough?

Some charter-granting agencies (notably the Massachusetts state board of education, the District of Columbia Public Charter School Board, and the Chicago Public Schools) have developed detailed policies on these issues, but many others have not. Thus, from the public's point of view, the degree to which charter schools will truly be held accountable for performance is unclear. Until charter-granting agencies have policies in place that define charter schools' accountability for results, taxpayers cannot feel confident that the bargain of autonomy for accountability is working. From the perspective of charter schools, the absence of clear accountability systems makes it difficult to act decisively in the development of their schools. And uncertainty about how they will be judged presents problems for charter schools when they approach lenders and landlords about undertaking long-term obligations. If the charter renewal process is cloaked in mystery, lenders and landlords have trouble evaluating the risk of offering loans or leases to charter schools, a problem that exacerbates already severe facilities problems.

Consequently, both the public at large and individual charter schools have a direct interest in the development of systems for holding charter schools accountable for results. More indirectly, the broader public school system might benefit from the work charter-granting agencies do to develop these systems. Public school districts and state education agencies everywhere are struggling with how to hold schools accountable for results. As Chapter 6 suggested, charter school programs are potential laboratories for finding answers to these questions.

Accountability for Compliance

Though free from many laws and regulations, even charter schools in states with the strongest laws are subject to some restrictions. These fall into three categories. First, charter schools remain subject to federal law, which state charter laws, of course, cannot waive. Charter schools must provide a "free and appropriate public education" to children with special needs, respect students' constitutional rights, maintain nondiscriminatory policies in admission and other areas, and refrain from teaching religion. Second, most charter school laws leave at least some state-level school law in place for charter schools. For example, some charter laws require charter schools to hire only certified teachers or to meet regular state reporting requirements for student attendance and finances. Third, some charter laws impose requirements that are unique to charter schools. For example, some state laws require each school to submit an annual report on its activities. Others require that the student body of each charter school replicates the demographic characteristics of its surrounding district.

As discussed in Chapter 4, even charter schools in states with relatively strong laws have reported that a great deal of their leadership's attention has been devoted to handling the details of administration required by residual regulation. Recall that residual regulation in states with strong laws has not kept charter schools from choosing their own paths in the areas that matter most, like what to teach and how to spend money. Rather, residual regulation's main effect has been to divert schools' attention and resources away from these more critical responsibilities. Without district bureaucracies to rely upon, charter schools must fulfill a host of reporting requirements and carry out other compliance activities on their own.

As the infrastructure of support develops, charter schools receive more help in handling these requirements. But a more effective way to relieve charter schools of these burdens may be for chartering authorities to rethink how they ensure that charter schools comply with the laws and regulations. Simply including charter schools in pre-existing systems of monitoring and enforcement is not sufficient. These systems were designed on the assumption that central school district bureaucracies, not individual schools, would be responsible for compliance. Since districts can spread the costs over a large number of schools and students, they can afford to hire specialized staff who become well versed in the arcane details of fulfilling a specific requirement or completing a given report. Since charter schools cannot do that, the burdens of complying with these systems are often much greater than those shouldered by conventional schools.

Chartering authorities could relieve this burden by rebuilding reporting and compliance systems from the ground up for charter schools.

They could begin by asking what information an agency truly needs to fulfill its obligations under the law and then design systems accordingly. In isolated cases, regulatory authorities have taken this approach with charter schools, with good results. In Massachusetts, for example, charter schools do not have to engage in the same financial reporting activities that regular districts carry out. Instead, schools submit monthly reports to the state department that include financial statements, annual reports summing up the year's activity, and annual external audits of their finances. This streamlined system gives state officials most of the information they need to evaluate charter schools' spending patterns. And if they have further questions, they can always conduct additional audits. At the same time, the system places a minimal burden on charter schools. The monthly reports they are required to prepare contain information school leaders would probably pull together in any case for their own management purposes.

Retooling administrative systems in this way would be of great benefit to charter schools. But the potential prize is larger than that. By experimenting with new ways of gathering information from schools and ensuring compliance with critical laws and regulations, regulators may begin to develop models of monitoring and enforcement that fulfill public obligations while placing lighter burdens on schools. If these models work in the charter school environment, there is no reason why they could not be exported to more conventional public schools as well.

Conclusion

For charter schools to have a positive impact on public education as a whole, policymakers will need go back to the drawing boards of charter school legislation. Charter schools and those who support them will need to develop an infrastructure of support that allows charter schools to focus on teaching and learning while remaining viable as enterprises. And regulators will need to retool systems of oversight to ensure accountability while minimizing the administrative burdens on this new form of independent public school. None of these tasks will be easy. But charter schools have already established a reputation for forging ahead even under the most difficult circumstances. They have surprised many by surviving in less-than-ideal physical surroundings and despite philosophical opposition; in that regard, at least, they stand out as a compelling example to all involved in the enterprise of public education. Perhaps despite the host of political and operational challenges they face, charter schools will surprise skeptics yet again.

Notes

Chapter One

1. Center for Education Reform, "Charter School Highlights and Statistics," published on the center's website: http://edreform.com.

2. Rene Sanchez, "Embracing New Schools of Thought; States Charter Independent Institutions to Improve Public Education," *Washington Post*, December 5, 1995, p. A1; Claudia Wallis, "A Class of Their Own," *Time*, October 31, 1994, p. 53; Drew Lindsey, "Laws of the Land: Are Charters an Idea Whose Time Has Come and Gone?" in "Breaking Away," *Education Week*, special section, November 29, 1995, p. 8; Chris Pipho, "Stateline," *Phi Delta Kappan*, vol. 76 (June 1995), p. 742.

3. Lindsey, "Laws of the Land," p. 8.

4. Ray Budde, *Education by Charter: Restructuring School Districts* (Andover, Mass.: Regional Laboratory for Educational Improvement of the Northeast and the Islands, 1988).

5. Michelle Fine, ed., *Chartering Urban School Reform: Reflections on Public High Schools in the Midst of Change* (New York: Teachers College Press, 1994).

6. Priscilla Wohlstetter and Lesley Anderson, "What Can U.S. Charter Schools Learn from England's Grant-Maintained Schools?" *Phi Delta Kappan*, vol. 75 (February 1994), pp. 486–89.

7. A comprehensive review of the literature on all of these proposed reforms is beyond the scope of this introduction. This footnote lists a few key references for each: (1) Choice: Early treatments from a variety of ideological perspectives include Milton Friedman, *Capitalism and Freedom* (University of Chicago Press, 1962), chap. 6, pp. 85–107;

Henry M. Levin, "The Failure of the Public School and the Free Market Remedy," *Urban Review*, vol. 2, no. 7 (1968), pp. 32–37; Mario D. Fantini, *Public Schools of Choice* (Simon and Schuster, 1973); John E. Coons and Stephen D. Sugarman, *Education by Choice: The Case for Family Control* (University of California Press, 1978). There are several more recent book-length arguments for and against wide-reaching school choice as well as edited volumes and articles with differing views: John E. Chubb and Terry M. Moe, *Politics, Markets, and America's Schools* (The Brookings Institution, 1990) Jeffrey R. Henig, *Rethinking School Choice: Limits of the Market Metaphor* (Princeton University Press, 1994); Peter W. Cookson Jr., *School Choice: The Struggle for the Soul of American Education* (Yale University Press, 1994); William H. Clune and John F. Witte, eds., *Choice and Control in American Education*, vol. 1: *The Theory of Choice and Control in Education* (London: Falmer, 1990); Clune and Witte, eds., *Choice and Control in American Education*, vol. 2: *The Practice of Choice, Decentralization and School Restructuring* (London: Falmer, 1990); Edith Rasell and Richard Rothstein, eds., *School Choice: Examining the Evidence* (Washington: Economic Policy Institute, 1993); Peter W. Cookson Jr., ed., *The Choice Controversy* (Newbury Park, Calif.: Corwin, 1992); Bruce Fuller, Richard Elmore, and Gary Orfield, eds., *Who Chooses? Who Loses? Culture, Institutions, and the Unequal Effects of School Choice* (New York: Teachers College Press, 1996); Paul Peterson and Bryan Hassel, eds., *Learning from School Choice* (The Brookings Institution, 1998). (2) Monopoly: Most writing about the school-system monopoly appears in the literature on choice. See also Paul Peterson, "Monopoly and Competition in American Education," in Clune and Witte, eds., *Choice and Control in American Education*, vol. 1; Paul Hill, *Reinventing Education* (Santa Monica, Calif.: Rand, 1995), pp. 47–78. (3) School-based management: For an overview of the research, see Betty Malen, Rodney T. Ogawa, and Jennifer Kranz, "What Do We Know about School-Based Management? A Case Study of the Literature—A Call for Research," in Clune and Witte, eds., *Choice and Control in American Education*, vol. 2, pp. 289–342. (4) Deregulation: See Susan H. Fuhrman and Richard F. Elmore, *Ruling Out Rules: The Evolution of Deregulation in State Education Policy* (New Brunswick, N.J.: Consortium for Policy Research in Education, 1995). (5) Accountability for results: see Helen F. Ladd, ed., *Holding Schools Accountable: Performance-Based Reform in Education* (The Brookings Institution, 1996).

8. Paraphrased from Ted Kolderie, *Beyond Choice to New Public Schools: Withdrawing the Exclusive Franchise in Public Education* (Washington: Progressive Policy Institute, 1990).

9. Ted Kolderie, *The States Begin to Withdraw the Exclusive*, Public Services Redesign Project (St. Paul, Minn.: Center for Policy Studies, 1993).

10. For a more detailed explanation, see Bryan Hassel, "The Charter School Idea: Elements of an Effective Charter School Program," Taubman Center Working Paper Series (John F. Kennedy School of Government, Harvard University, 1995).

11. Kolderie, *The States Begin to Withdraw the Exclusive*, p. 1.

12. Craig Sautter, *Charter Schools: A New Breed of Public Schools* (Oak Brook, Ill.: North Central Regional Education Laboratory, 1993).

13. Chubb and Moe, *Politics, Markets, and America's Schools.*

14. See, for example, Louann Bierlein and Lori Mulholland, *Charter Schools: A Viable Reform Initiative* (Tempe, Ariz.: Morrison Institute for Public Policy, 1992); Louann Bierlein and Lori Mulholland, *Charter School Update: Expansion of a Viable Reform Initiative* (Tempe, Ariz.: Morrison Institute for Public Policy, 1993); Marcella R. Dianda

and Ronald G. Corwin, *An Early Look at Charter Schools in California* (Los Alamitos, Calif.: Southwest Regional Laboratory, 1993); Marcella R. Dianda and Ronald G. Corwin, *Vision and Reality: A First-Year Look at California's Charter Schools* (Los Alamitos, Calif.: Southwest Regional Laboratory, 1994); Lori Mulholland and Mary Amsler, *The Search for Choice in Public Education: The Emergence of Charter Schools* (San Francisco: Far West Laboratory for Educational Research and Development, 1992); Sautter, *Charter Schools: A New Breed of Public Schools*; Marc Dean Millot, *Autonomy, Accountability, and the Values of Public Education: A Comparative Assessment of Charter School Strategies Leading to Model Legislation* (Washington: Rand, 1994); Mark Buechler, *Charter Schools: Legislation and Results after Four Years* (Bloomington: Indiana Education Policy Center, 1996).

15. Ted Kolderie, Robert Lerman, and Charles Moskos, "Educating America: A New Compact for Opportunity and Citizenship," in Will Marshall and Martin Schram, eds., *Mandate for Change* (New York: Berkley Books, 1993), pp. 129–51.

16. Joe Nathan, *Charter Schools: Creating Hope and Opportunity for American Education* (San Francisco: Jossey-Bass, 1996).

17. See, for example, Millot, *Autonomy, Accountability, and the Values of Public Education*; Priscilla Wohlstetter, Richard Wenning, and Kerri L. Briggs, "Charter Schools in the United States: The Question of Autonomy," *Educational Policy*, vol. 9 (December 1995), pp. 331–58; Louann Bierlein and Lori Mulholland, *Comparing Charter School Laws: The Issue of Autonomy* (Tempe, Ariz.: Morrison Institute for Public Policy, 1994); American Federation of Teachers, *Charter School Laws: Do They Measure Up?* (Washington, 1996).

18. U.S. General Accounting Office, *Charter Schools: New Model for Public Schools Provides Opportunities and Challenges* (Washington, 1995).

19. Chester E. Finn Jr., Bruno V. Manno, and Louann Bierlein, *Charter Schools in Action: What Have We Learned?* (Washington: Hudson Institute, 1996). Follow-up study: Chester E. Finn Jr., Bruno V. Manno, Louann Bierlein, and Gregg Vanourek, *Charter Schools in Action: A Final Report* (Washington: Hudson Institute, 1997).

20. For example, see Amy Stewart Wells, *Beyond the Rhetoric of Charter School Reform* (Los Angeles: UCLA Graduate School of Education and Information Sciences, 1998); Ronald G. Corwin and John F. Flaherty, eds., *Freedom and Innovation in California's Charter Schools* (Los Alamitos, Calif.: Southwest Regional Laboratory, 1995); SRI International, *Evaluation of Charter School Effectiveness* [California] (Sacramento, Calif.: Office of the Legislative Analyst, 1997); Clayton Foundation, *1997 Colorado Charter Schools Evaluation Study: The Characteristics, Status and Student Achievement Data of Colorado Charter Schools* (Denver, Colo.: Colorado Department of Education, 1997); Rosenblum Brigham Associates, *Innovation and Massachusetts Charter Schools* (Boston, Mass.: Massachusetts Department of Education, 1998); Sue Urahn and Dan Stewart, *Minnesota Charter Schools: A Research Report* (Minneapolis: Minnesota House of Representatives Research Department, 1994); Center for Applied Research and Educational Improvement, *Minnesota Charter Schools Evaluation: Interim Report.* (Minneapolis: CAREI, 1996); Delbert Taebel, Edith J. Barret, Christine T. Brenner, and others, *Texas Open-Enrollment Charter Schools: Year One Evaluation* (Austin: Texas State Board of Education, 1997).

21. RPP International and the University of Minnesota, *A Study of Charter Schools* (Washington: U.S. Office of Educational Research and Improvement, 1997); RPP International, *A National Study of Charter Schools: Second-Year Report* (Washington: U.S. Office of Educational Research and Improvement, 1998).

22. Effects on local schools: Eric Rofes, *How Are School Districts Responding to Charter Laws and Charter Schools?* (Policy Analysis for California Education, University of California at Berkeley, 1998). Student achievement and accountability: Stella Cheung, Mary Ellen S. Murphy, and Joe Nathan, *Making a Difference? Charter Schools, Evaluation, and Student Performance* (Center for School Change, University of Minnesota, 1998).

23. RPP International, *A National Study of Charter Schools* [1998], p. 59.

24. Ibid., pp. 35, 48, 53, 56, 59. By "distinctively higher," the study means that the percentage of nonwhite students in the charter school is at least 20 percent higher than the percentage in the schools of the surrounding district.

25. Louann A. Bierlein, "Existing Charter School Laws: Analysis of 'Stronger' Components," mimeograph, 1995.

26. Angela Dale and David DeSchryver, eds., *The Charter School Workbook: Your Roadmap to the Charter School Movement* (Washington: Center for Education Reform, 1997); Michael Mintrom and Sandra Vergari, *Michigan's Charter Schools Initiative: A Comparative Analysis* (Institute for Public Policy and Social Research, Michigan State University, 1995).

27. RPP International and the University of Minnesota, *A Study of Charter Schools*, 1997, p. 7; RPP International, *A National Study of Charter Schools*, 1998, p. 92.

Chapter Two

1. Louann A. Bierlein, "Existing Charter School Laws: Analysis of 'Stronger' Components," mimeograph, 1995; Louann A. Bierlein, *Charter Schools: Initial Findings* (Denver: Education Commission of the States, 1996); Ted Kolderie, *The Charter Idea: Update and Prospects, Fall '95*, Public Services Redesign Project (St. Paul, Minn.: Center for Policy Studies, 1995).

2. This book uses the terms "strong" and "weak" to distinguish different types of charter laws. This terminology, of course, reflects the perspective of charter school advocates. Opponents of charter schools do not regard "strong" laws as strong at all. Because of the prevalence of these terms, however, the strong-weak distinction provides the most straightforward way to differentiate the types of laws.

3. For a more detailed discussion of these issues, see Bryan Hassel, "The Charter School Idea: Elements of an Effective Charter School Program," Taubman Center Working Paper Series (John F. Kennedy School of Government, Harvard University, 1995). For other analyses of state laws that include more than the initial 20 statutes, see Angela Dale and David DeSchryver, eds., *The Charter School Workbook: Your Roadmap to the Charter School Movement* (Washington: Center for Education Reform, 1997), chap. 2; RPP International, *A National Study of Charter Schools: Second-Year Report* (Washington: U.S. Office of Educational Research and Improvement, 1998), pp. 13–25 and appendix B.

4. In Texas, the duration of the charter is not specified in the charter law; each charter contract sets out its own duration.

5. Bierlein, "Existing Charter School Laws"; Kolderie, *The Charter Idea*.

6. John F. Bibby and Thomas M. Holbrook, "Parties and Elections," in Virginia Gray and Herbert Jacob, eds., *Politics in the American States: A Comparative Analysis*, 6th ed. (Washington: CQ Press, 1996), pp. 105–6.

7. Austin Ranney, "Parties in State Politics," in Herbert Jacob and Kenneth Vines, eds., *Politics in the American States: A Comparative Analysis*, 3d ed. (Boston: Little, Brown, 1976); Thomas R. Dye, "Party and Policy in the States," *Journal of Politics*, vol. 46 (November 1984), pp. 1097–1116.

8. Catherine Marshall, Douglas Mitchell, and Frederick Wirt, *Culture and Education Policy in the American States* (New York: Falmer, 1989).

9. Larry Sabato, *Goodbye to Good-Time Charlie: The American Governorship Transformed* (Lexington, Mass.: Lexington Books, 1978); Thad Beyle, "Being Governor," in Carl E. Van Horn, ed., *The State of the States*, 3d ed. (Washington: CQ Press, 1996); Thad Beyle, "Governors: The Middlemen and Women in Our Political System," in Gray and Jacob, *Politics in the American States*; Thad Beyle, "The Governor as Innovator in the Federal System," *Publius: The Journal of Federalism*, vol. 18 (Summer 1988), pp. 131–52.

10. Margaret E. Goertz, "State Education Policy in the 1990's," in Carl E. Van Horn, ed., *The State of the States*, 3d ed. (Washington: CQ Press, 1996).

11. Kolderie, *The Charter Idea*; Chris Pipho, "Bipartisan Charter Schools," *Phi Delta Kappan*, vol. 75 (October 1993), pp. 102–3.

12. This broad-brush characterization of partisan positions, of course, masks significant differences within the parties. Within the Democratic Party, moderate elements associated with the Democratic Leadership Council (DLC) have been early advocates for strong legislation. The DLC, in fact, published one of the first charter school manifestos, Ted Kolderie's *Beyond Choice to New Public Schools: Withdrawing the Exclusive Franchise in Public Education* (Washington: Progressive Policy Institute, 1990). Within the Republican Party, certain conservative factions have opposed charter schools. Market true-believers have argued that charter schools do not go far enough toward the system of choice and competition they favor; religious fundamentalists and some back-to-basics advocates also worry that charter school programs will foster exactly the sort of educational experimentation they despise.

13. Clive S. Thomas and Ronald J. Hrebenar, "Interest Groups in the States," in Gray and Jacob, *Politics in the American States*, pp. 122–58.

14. Stephen K. Bailey, Richard T. Frost, Paul E. Marsh, and Robert C. Wood, *Schoolmen and Politics: A Study of State Aid to Education in New England* (Syracuse University Press, 1962).

15. Fragmentation: Laurence Iannacone, *State Politics of Education* (New York: Center for Applied Research in Education, 1967); Roald F. Campbell and Tim L. Mazzoni Jr., *State Policy Making for the Public Schools: A Comparative Analysis of Policy Making for the Public Schools in Twelve States and a Treatment of State Governance Models* (Berkeley, Calif.: McCutchan, 1976); Joel Spring, *Conflict of Interests* (New York: Longman, 1988); Frederick M. Wirt and Michael W. Kirst, *Schools in Conflict*, 2d ed. (Berkeley, Calif.: McCutchan, 1989), chaps. 4 and 5. Collective action: Jane H. Karper and William Lowe Boyd, "Interest Groups and the Changing Environment of State Educational Policymaking: Developments in Pennsylvania," *Educational Administration Quarterly*, vol. 24 (February 1988), pp. 21–54; Michael W. Kirst and Stephen A. Somers, "California Educational Interest Groups: Collective Action as a Logical Response to Proposition 13," *Education and Urban Society*, vol. 13 (February 1981), pp. 235–56.

16. See Bailey, Frost, March, and Wood, *Schoolmen and Politics*; Thomas and Hrebenar, "Interest Groups in the States," pp. 122–58.

17. See American Federation of Teachers, *Charter School Laws: Do They Measure Up?* (Washington, 1996), which cites Rhode Island's law as a model charter statute.

18. Daniel J. Elazar, *American Federalism: A View from the States*, 3d ed. (Harper and Row, 1984). Among the applications of these categories to education policymaking are: Catherine Marshall, Douglas Mitchell, and Frederick Wirt, *Culture and Education Policy in the American States* (New York: Falmer, 1989); Susan H. Fuhrman, "State Politics and Education Reform," in Jane Hannaway and Robert Crowson, eds., *The Politics of Reforming School Administration: The 1988 Yearbook of the Politics of Education Association* (New York: Falmer, 1989).

19. Jack L. Walker Jr., "The Diffusion of Innovations among the American States," *American Political Science Review*, vol. 63 (September 1969), pp. 880–99; Virginia Gray, "Innovations in the States: A Diffusion Study," *American Political Science Review*, vol. 67 (December 1973), pp. 1174–85.

20. It is also possible to determine whether the observed differences are statistically significant by conducting a test of "the equality of independent proportions"; see Richard J. Larsen and Morris L. Marx, *An Introduction to Mathematical Statistics and Its Applications*, 2d ed.(Englewood Cliffs, N.J.: Prentice-Hall, 1986), pp. 378–80). The discussion treats a difference as important only if it met standards of statistical significance. Full details of this procedure and the test statistics from this analysis can be found in Bryan Hassel, "Designed to Fail? Charter Schools and the Politics of Structural Choice," Ph.D. diss., Harvard University, 1997.

21. Across the board, Democratic control is fairly common. Of the 245 state-years in the period 1991–95 (five for each state, excluding nonpartisan Nebraska), Democrats controlled both houses of the legislature and the governorship in 72 state-years.

22. Membership data for 1991 from American Federation of Teachers, "Membership by State," mimeograph (Washington: American Federation of Teachers, 1998), and National Education Association, *NEA Handbook* (Washington, 1991–92), table 2. Population data for 1991 from U.S. Bureau of the Census, "Estimates of the Population of States: Annual Time Series, July 1, 1990, to July 1, 1997" (Washington, 1997).

23. The analysis uses 1992 data because 41 of the 50 states participated in that year, many more than in 1990. The NAEP math test includes several content areas; this analysis uses pooled scores for all content areas. Data used for this analysis were derived from NAEP's revised figures, which reflect corrections made in 1996. National Assessment of Educational Progress, "Revised Mathematics Assessment Data for Grade 8," published on NAEP's website: http://www.ed.gov.NCES/naep.

24. A similar analysis that examined the Scholastic Aptitude Test (SAT) rather than NAEP showed that higher- and lower-performing states on the SAT were equally likely to pass charter laws. And though lower-performing states were slightly more likely to pass strong laws, the difference was not statistically significant.

25. Elazar, *American Federalism*.

26. Ibid., p. 137.

27. The income measure is median household income for a state in 1990; see U.S. Bureau of the Census, *Current Population Reports*, series P-60 (Washington: U.S. Government Printing Office, 1996), table H-8. Urbanization is the percentage of residents living in urban areas in 1990; see U.S. Bureau of the Census, "Population and Housing Unit Counts, CPH 2-1," *1990 Census of Population and Housing* (Washington: U.S. Gov-

ernment Printing Office, 1995), table 1. Household income in states ranged from $20,178 to $40,805, with a median of $29,253. The percentage of residents in urban areas ranges from 32.2 percent to 92.6 percent, with a median of 68.8 percent.

28. Instead of regarding states as observations, one could regard state-years as observations. Such a procedure would increase the "n" from 50 to 228 and enable a more sophisticated analysis. The problem with this technique is that the only independent variables that change significantly from year to year within a state are partisan control and, to a lesser extent, educational conditions. The others—union membership and the various measures of culture—either remain constant or are not measured each year.

29. Union strength was included because, among the variables that appeared insignificant in the bivariate analyses, union strength carries the most theoretical importance, since unions are typically among the most vocal opponents of charter legislation. Other analyses, not reported here, included the other nonsignificant variables (indicators of educational conditions) and found that (1) they remained insignificant and (2) their inclusion did not affect inferences about the importance of the other variables.

30. These results derive from two probit analyses, one in which the dependent variable was the passage of a charter law by January 1996, and one in which it was passage of a strong charter law by January 1996. Independent variables included a composite variable summarizing the degree of control held by Republicans in both the legislature and the governorship; a composite of income and urbanization; a variable indicating a moralistic political culture; and the measure of the strength of the unions used in Table 2-2. Full details of the construction of variables and the results of the models are available in Hassel, "Designed to Fail?"

Chapter Three

1. National Center for Education Statistics, *The Condition of Education 1996* (Washington: U.S. Government Printing Office, 1996), p. 47.

2. These conflicts are not always between urban and rural districts. Often, the two join forces, implicitly challenging wealthier suburban districts. Typically, though, rural interests are a driving force in court and political battles over school finance.

3. Perhaps the most widely read call for these reforms was written by David Osborne and Ted Gaebler, *Reinventing Government: How the Entrepreneurial Spirit Is Transforming the Public Sector* (Reading, Mass.: Addison-Wesley, 1992). The nation's first charter state, Minnesota, was also on the cutting edge of these developments more generally; see Michael Barzelay with Babak Armajani, *Breaking through Bureaucracy: A New Vision for Managing in Government* (University of California Press, 1992). Similar proposals were under consideration in the national government; see Al Gore, *From Red Tape to Results: Creating a Government That Works Better and Costs Less* (New York: Plume, 1993). And countries around the world (notably Great Britain, New Zealand, and Australia) were experimenting with a range of dramatic reforms in their public sectors; see Donald J. Savoie, *Thatcher, Reagan, Mulroney: In Search of a New Bureaucracy* (University of Pittsburgh Press, 1994); Christopher Hood, "A Public Management for All Seasons?" *Public Administration*, vol. 69, no. 1 (1991), pp. 3–19; Colin Campbell and John Halligan, *Political Leadership in an Age of Constraint: The Australian Experience* (University of Pitts-

burgh Press, 1992); Colin Campbell and Graham K. Wilson, *The End of Whitehall: Death of a Paradigm?* (Oxford: Blackwell, 1995); Jonathan Boston, John Martin, June Pallot, and Pat Walsh, *Public Management: The New Zealand Model* (Auckland: Oxford University Press, 1996).

4. Great Britain allowed public schools to withdraw from their local public systems and operate independently, with direct funding from the central government. New Zealand and Victoria province in Australia reformed their education systems along charter-like lines as well. See Priscilla Wohlstetter and Lesley Anderson, "What Can U.S. Charter Schools Learn from England's Grant-Maintained Schools?" *Phi Delta Kappan,* vol. 75 (February 1994), pp. 486–91; Allan Odden and Carolyn Busch, *Financing Schools for High Performance: Strategies for Improving the Use of Educational Resources* (San Francisco: Jossey-Bass, 1998).

5. For an excellent account of these networks and how they influenced the diffusion of charter legislation, see Michael Mintrom and Sandra Vergari, "Why Policy Innovations Change as They Diffuse: Analyzing Recent Charter School Laws," paper presented at the 1997 Annual Meeting of the Midwest Political Science Association, Chicago, April 10, 1997.

6. The DLC published one of the initial charter school manifestos, Ted Kolderie's *Beyond Choice to New Public Schools: Withdrawing the Exclusive Franchise in Public Education* (Washington: Progressive Policy Institute, 1990). The NGA did not promote charter schools per se in this period, but its *Time for Results* publication advocated many of the policy instruments involved in charter legislation; see National Governors Association, *Time for Results: The Governors' 1991 Report on Education* (Washington, 1986).

7. In Mintrom and Vergari's survey of state policymakers and observers, respondents in states with strong charter laws were likely to cite ECS and NCLS as sources of information; Mintrom and Vergari, "Why Policy Innovations Change," p. 9.

8. For an account of the national teachers' associations' activities regarding charter schools, see Joe Nathan, *Charter Schools: Creating Hope and Opportunity for American Education* (San Francisco: Jossey-Bass, 1996), chap. 4, pp. 93–118.

9. American Federation of Teachers, "American Federation of Teachers Membership by State," November 1998, mimeograph; National Association of Educators, *NEA Handbook* (Washington, 1991–92), table 2; U.S. Bureau of the Census, Population Division, "Estimates of the Population of States: Annual Time Series, July 1, 1990 to July 1, 1997" (Washington, 1997).

10. U.S. General Accounting Office, *School Finance: State Efforts to Reduce Funding Gaps between Wealthy and Poor Districts* (Washington, 1997), pp. 184–88.

11. Sandra Vergari, "School Finance Reform in the State of Michigan," *Journal of Educational Finance,* vol. 21 (1995), pp. 254–70.

12. Chris Christoff, "Stabenow Unveils Plan for Schools," *Detroit Free Press,* September 16, 1993, sec. C.

13. Chris Christoff, "Activist Group Wants Right to Shop Around," *Detroit Free Press,* September 3, 1993, sec. B; interview with Paul DeWeese, executive director, TEACH Michigan. All interviews were conducted by the author.

14. John Engler, "Our Kids Deserve Better! New Schools for a New Century," mimeograph issued by Office of the Governor of Michigan, 1993; Chris Christoff and Dawson Bell, "Engler Must Build Coalition to Pass Bold School Changes," *Detroit Free Press,* October 5, 1993, sec. A.

15. Vergari, "School Finance Reform," p. 262.

16. Michigan Senate Bill 896 (1993), as introduced, p.4, lines 7–19.

17. Michigan Senate Bill 896 (1993), as introduced, p. 2, line 22, to p. 3, line 2.

18. Dawson Bell, "MEA Donations Lead Class," *Detroit Free Press,* November 15, 1993, sec. A.

19. Interview with DeWeese; interview with Richard McClellan, the attorney who drafted the initial charter legislation in Michigan.

20. Joan Richardson, "Teachers Union Draws Its Reform Terms," *Detroit Free Press,* August 25, 1993, sec. B.

21. Joan Richardson, "MEA Seeks War Chest in Fighting School Plan," *Detroit Free Press,* November 5, 1993, sec. B.

22. Joan Richardson, "Business Execs Back Engler's School Plan," *Detroit Free Press,* November 12, 1993, sec. A.

23. Bell, "MEA Donations Lead Class."

24. Chris Christoff, "Legislators Say What Needs Fixing Isn't Their Schools," *Detroit Free Press,* November 3, 1993, sec. B.

25. Richardson, "Teachers Union Draws Its Reform Terms."

26. Chris Christoff, "Engler: Schools Deserve Better; Sales Tax Hike, Choice of Districts Face Fight," *Detroit Free Press,* October 6, 1993, sec. A; Chris Christoff, "House Breaks School Logjam," *Detroit Free Press,* November 30, 1993, sec. A.

27. Joe Stroud, "Key Issues Should Shape School Debate," *Detroit Free Press,* October 10, 1993, sec. F; Richardson, "MEA Seeks War Chest in Fighting School Plan."

28. Interview with Al Short, chief lobbyist, Michigan Education Association; interview with Cynthia Irwin, chief counsel, Michigan Education Association.

29. Debra Adams, Lori Montgomery, and Margaret Trimer-Hartley, "How It Would Work and How It's Playing; Educators, Parents Grade Financing Formula," *Detroit Free Press,* October 6, 1993, sec. A.

30. Chris Christoff, "Real School Battle Will Be Choice: Funding May Play Second Fiddle," *Detroit Free Press,* November 8, 1993, sec. B.

31. Chris Christoff and Joan Richardson, "Engler Plan for Schools Splits Critics," *Detroit Free Press,* October 1, 1993, sec. A; interview with Justin King, executive director, Michigan Association of School Boards.

32. Interviews with Short, Irwin, and King.

33. Vergari, "School Finance Reform," pp. 254–70.

34. Michigan Senate Bill 896 (1993), as approved by Senate Education Committee (known as S-2).

35. *Journal of the Senate 1993,* pp. 2727–28; 2784–27; 2797–99.

36. Michigan Senate Bill 896 (1993), as approved by the Senate.

37. Interview with McClellan.

38. Several senators, however, did make reference on the Senate floor to the furious negotiating that preceded the final agreement. See *Journal of the Senate 1993,* pp. 3039–40. Interviews with Short, Irwin, and McClellan informed this account. For the original bill text, see Michigan House Bill 5124 (1993), as introduced.

39. Michigan House Bill 5124 (1993), as approved by House Education Committee (known as H-3), p. 5, lines 3–24.

40. Ibid., p. 14, line 1, to p. 15, line 8.

41. Christoff, "House Breaks School Logjam."

42. American Federation of Teachers, "American Federation of Teachers Membership by State"; National Association of Educators, *NEA Handbook,* table 2; U.S. Bureau of the Census, Population Division, "Estimates of the Population of States."

43. Muriel Cohen, "Revival Sought of Lawsuit on Inequities in School Funding," *Boston Globe,* March 11, 1996, sec. A.

44. Anthony Flint and Muriel Cohen, "Teacher Unions, Others Criticize School Package," *Boston Globe,* November 27, 1991. McDuffy was the new plaintiff (the original plaintiff had since graduated from school); Robertson is Piedad Robertson, Governor William Weld's appointee to the now defunct cabinet position, secretary of education.

45. U.S. General Accounting Office, *School Finance: State Efforts to Reduce Funding Gaps between Wealthy and Poor Districts* (Washington: GAO, 1997), pp. 179–83.

46. Anthony Flint, "Democrats Unveil Plan for School Reform; Could Cost $1b, Kill Decrease in State Income Tax," *Boston Globe,* November 26, 1991; Muriel Cohen, "A Plan That, Given Funding, Might Have Consensus to Take Off," *Boston Globe,* November 26, 1991.

47. Flint and Cohen, "Teacher Unions, Others Criticize School Package."

48. Richard Fossey, "Open Enrollment in Massachusetts: Why Families Choose," *Educational Evaluation and Policy Analysis,* vol. 16 (Fall 1994), pp. 320–34.

49. Flint, "Democrats Unveil Plan for School Reform"; Cohen, "A Plan That, Given Funding, Might Have Consensus to Take Off."

50. Muriel Cohen, "School Bill Stalled by Question of Pupil Costs," *Boston Globe,* April 9, 1992.

51. Cohen, "A Plan That, Given Funding, Might Have Consensus to Take Off."

52. Flint, "Democrats Unveil Plan for School Reform." Analyses of Massachusetts state politics have characterized it as "individualistic" in that ad hoc coalitions of legislators hold more sway than political parties; see John C. Berg, "Massachusetts: Citizen Power and Corporate Power," in Ronald J. Hrebenar and Clive S. Thomas, eds., *Interest Group Politics in the Northeastern States* (Pennsylvania State University Press, 1993), pp. 167–97. Education reform politics in 1993, with key Democratic legislators endorsing policies opposed by key party constituencies, appears to fit this pattern.

53. Muriel Cohen, "Business Leaders Tackle Schools," *Boston Globe,* January 23, 1992.

54. Wilson became one of Weld's key policy advisers.

55. Steven F. Wilson, *Reinventing the Schools: A Radical Plan for Boston* (Boston: Pioneer Institute, 1992), p. 86.

56. Flint and Cohen, "Teacher Unions, Others Criticize School Package."

57. Jordana Hart, "A Breed Apart; Experimental Schools Vying for State OK," *Boston Globe,* February 9, 1994; Victoria Benning, "Charters Awarded for 15 Schools," *Boston Globe,* March 19, 1994.

58. Berg, "Massachusetts: Citizen Power and Corporate Power," p. 198.

59. In his review of interest group politics in Massachusetts, Berg notes that in light of long-standing Democratic dominance of the state legislature, labor had hitched its political fortunes almost exclusively to the Democratic wagon. Ibid.

60. Muriel Cohen, "Teacher Unions Back School Reform Ideas," *Boston Globe,* March 27, 1992.

61. Muriel Cohen, "Mass. Teachers Threaten to Strike; Action Would Protest Budget Shortages," *Boston Globe,* May 12, 1992; Teresa M. Hanafin, "School Reform Proposal Revised; Some Funds Would Aid Richer," *Boston Globe,* May 13, 1992.

62. Peter J. Howe, "Weld Said to Be Filing School Plan; Reportedly Moved by Bipartisan Failure," *Boston Globe,* June 2, 1992.

63. "Pitting Business against Schools," editorial, *Boston Globe,* July 15, 1992.

64. Teresa M. Hanafin, "Lawmakers Override Weld on School Aid," *Boston Globe,* July 29, 1992.

65. Massachusetts HB 800 (1993), lines 44–45 and 32, inter alia.

66. Massachusetts HB 801 (1993), lines 47–48 and 32, inter alia.

67. Massachusetts HB 1000 (1993). For details of debates, see *Journal of the House* for January 26 and 27, 1993.

68. Massachusetts Senate Bill 1550 (1993), lines 30, 42–64, and 89–97, inter alia.

69. Massachusetts SB 1551 (1993). For details of databases, see *Journal of the Senate* 1993 for March 30, 1993.

70. Another late-hour compromise concerned the timing of the program's start. Proponents wanted to begin opening charter schools in the fall of 1994; negotiators ultimately agreed on a fall 1995 start to delay the fiscal impact on existing districts.

71. Teachers' union membership data from American Federation of Teachers, "American Federation of Teachers Membership by State"; National Association of Educators, *NEA Handbook,* table 2; U.S. Bureau of the Census, Population Division, "Estimates of the Population of States."

72. U.S. General Accounting Office, *School Finance: State Efforts to Reduce Funding Gaps between Wealthy and Poor Districts* (Washington, 1997), pp. 121–24.

73. Public School Finance Act (1988), Colo. Rev. Stat. 22-53-201 to 22-53-410.

74. Colorado House Bill 1299 (1992).

75. Interview with William Owen, former member, Colorado State Senate.

76. Colorado Department of Education, *A Report on Colorado School District Organization* (Denver: Colorado Department of Education, 1995), p. 1.

77. Interestingly, though, Colorado's original general laws in 1876 allowed any ten parents of school-age children to petition county superintendents for elections to establish new school districts. As a result of this provision, there were 2,105 school districts in the state by 1935. Many of those districts contained just a single school building, had a great deal of autonomy, and were initiated by groups of parents and thus resembled today's charter schools. Ibid., pp. 1–2.

78. "Colorado: Budget Problems Not as Bad as Predicted," *Daily Report Card,* June 29, 1993.

79. Council of State Governments, *The Book of the States 1992–1993* (Lexington, Ky., 1992); Council of State Governments, *State Elective Officials and the Legislatures 1993–1994* (Lexington, Ky., 1993).

80. "Up for Discussion: Colorado Reform Proposals," *Daily Report Card,* April 21, 1993.

81. Interview with Deborah Lynch, education adviser to the governor of Colorado.

82. Interviews with Owen and Lynch.

83. Interviews with Lynch and Owen.

84. Interview with Owen.

85. Richard Kraft, "Public Schools of Choice: Key to Colorado Education Reform," *Independence Issue Paper,* Working Paper 14-87 (Golden, Colo.: Independence Institute, 1987); David S. D'Evelyn, "School Choice: Not Yet Real in Colorado's Biggest District," *Independence Issue Paper,* Working Paper 11-89 (Golden, Colo.: Independence Institute, 1989).

86. "Colorado's Small-Business Owners Back House Bill Supporting Pay for Teachers," *PR Newswire,* February 25, 1993.

87. Colorado House Education Committee, Sound Recording of Hearings on Proposed Charter School Legislation, Denver, May 5, 1993.

88. Ibid.; Colorado Senate Education Committee, Sound Recording of Hearings on Proposed Charter School Legislation, Denver, February 4, 10, and 25 and March 4 and 18, 1993.

89. Ibid.

90. The smaller AFT-affiliated Colorado Federation of Teachers did not speak out so stridently against the bill. A January 1993 briefing paper distributed by the organization, for example, called for none of the restrictions advocated by the CEA and indeed appeared rather favorable toward the charter concept. Colorado Federation of Teachers, "Charter Schools" (Denver: Colorado Federation of Teachers, 1993, mimeograph).

91. Randy Quinn, "Charter Schools: Now What?" *CASB Agenda,* August 1993.

92. Interview with Randy Quinn, executive director, Colorado Association of School Boards.

93. Paul Brace and John A. Strayer, "Colorado: PACs, Political Candidates, and Conservatism," in Ronald J. Hrebenar and Clive S. Thomas, eds., *Interest Group Politics in the American West* (University of Utah Press, 1987), pp. 49–58.

94. Colorado Senate Bill 183 (1993), as introduced.

95. Joy Fitzgerald, *Charter Schools in Colorado* (Denver: Colorado Children's Campaign, 1995), p. 8.

96. Colorado Senate Bill 183 (1993), as approved by Senate Education Committee, p. 4, lines 15–17; p. 11, lines 21–24; p. 13, lines 6–8; p. 8, lines 22–25.

97. Colorado Senate Bill 183 (1993), as approved by Senate Education Committee, p. 10, lines 9–18; p. 5, line 23; p. 6, line 1; p. 14, lines 17–18.

98. Colorado Senate Bill 183 (1993), as approved by the Senate.

99. Colorado Senate Bill 183 (1993), as approved by the House, p. 15, lines 16–17; p. 5, lines 9–13.

100. Ibid., p. 11, lines 11–20.

101. Two of those voting yes were not identified by party in the *House Journal;* hence, "at least five." Colorado House of Representatives, *House Journal,* May 5, 1993, p. 1546.

102. Colorado Revised Statutes (1993), secs. 22–30.5, subsecs. 109(2)(a), 104(6), 112(2).

103. Ibid., subsec. 108.

104. Classifying Georgia's political culture is perhaps more complicated than Elazar's typology suggests. With one large urban center (Atlanta) as its hub surrounded by smaller towns and rural areas, Georgia arguably combines traditionalist elements with more individualist strands in Atlanta.

105. U.S. General Accounting Office, *School Finance: State Efforts to Reduce Funding Gaps between Wealthy and Poor Districts* (Washington, 1997), pp. 138–41.

106. Priscilla Wohlstetter, "Georgia: Reform at the Crossroads," in Diane Massell and Susan Fuhrman, eds., *Ten Years of State Education Reform, 1983–1993: Overview with Four Case Studies* (New Brunswick, N.J.: Consortium for Policy Research in Education, 1994).

107. Laura Wisniewski, "1993 Legislature," *Atlanta Journal and Constitution,* January 29, 1993.

108. Ibid.

109. Interview with Glenn Newsome, education adviser to the governor of Georgia.

110. Georgia Senate Bill 74 (1993), as introduced.

111. Charles S. Bullock III, *Georgia Political Almanac 1995–6* (Atlanta: Cornerstone, 1995), p. 52.

112. Interview with Kathleen Ashe, member, Georgia House of Representatives; Julie K. Miller, "Christian Soldiers: Fighting Mad about Their Perceived Assault on Family Values, Church Members Are Redoubling Their Efforts to Influence Legislation," *Atlanta Journal and Constitution,* April 20, 1993, sec. E.

113. Interview with Newsome.

114. Interview with Bill Barr, executive director, Georgia Association of School Superintendents.

115. Georgia Association of Educators, "Governor Miller's Education Legislation," mimeograph, 1993; Kay Pippin, "Georgia Charter Schools Legislation," memorandum to NEA Eastern States Government Relations Staff, Georgia Association of Educators, May 13, 1993; interview with Kay Pippin, government relations director, Georgia Association of Educators; interview with Robert Cribbs, government relations specialist, Georgia Association of Educators.

116. Eleanor C. Main, Lee Epstein, and Debra L. Elovich, "Georgia: Business as Usual," in Ronald J. Hrebenar and Clive S. Thomas, eds., *Interest Group Politics in the Southern States* (University of Alabama Press, 1992), pp. 231–48.

117. Georgia Senate Bill 74 (1993), as approved by the Senate, p. 3, lines 100–106; p. 4, lines 142–43; p. 4, lines 151–52; and p. 5, lines 166–67.

118. See *Journal of the Senate,* 1993, pp. 325–27; *Journal of the House,* 1993, pp. 1811–14.

119. For advocates of more far-reaching systems of school choice, of course, charter school laws are *already* a compromise, even in their ideal form.

Chapter Four

1. Eric Rofes, *How Are School Districts Responding to Charter Laws and Charter Schools?* (Policy Analysis for California Education, University of California at Berkeley, 1998); Joe Nathan, *Charter Schools: Creating Hope and Opportunity for American Education* (San Francisco: Jossey-Bass, 1996), pp. 85–92.

2. The first three sets of authorizers may only authorize schools within their own geographic territories, but universities may issue charters anywhere in the state. Michigan's intermediate school districts are essentially service-providing organizations for local school districts.

3. Subsequent legislation has shifted this power to the state board of education, which is also appointed by the governor. During the time frame of this study, however, the power rested with the secretary of education.

4. Georgia amended this provision in 1998 to allow outside groups to apply.

5. Data on number of charter schools per state from Colorado Department of Education, "Colorado Charter Schools. Charter Schools Approved and Operating," mimeograph, November 15, 1995; Massachusetts Department of Education, *The Massachusetts Charter School Initiative. 1996 Report* (Boston, 1996); Michigan Department of Educa-

tion, *A Description of Michigan Public School Academies. 1995–96 Report to the House and Senate Committees in Education* (Lansing, 1996); Georgia Department of Education, "Georgia Charter School Program. Annual Report Summaries. School Year 1996–97" [sic: actually 1995–96], mimeograph, ca.1996. Data on population per state in 1995 from U.S. Bureau of the Census, *1997 Statistical Abstract* (Washington: U.S. Bureau of the Census, 1998), table 26.

6. Colorado Department of Education, "Colorado Charter Schools. Charter Schools Approved and Operating," mimeograph, November 15, 1995; Colorado State Board of Education, "Charter Schools Status Report," memorandum, December 20, 1995.

7. Tom Loveless and Claudia Jasin, "Starting from Scratch: Political and Organizational Challenges Facing Charter Schools," *Educational Administration Quarterly*, vol. 34 (February 1998), pp. 9–30; interview with John Correiro, board member, Atlantis Charter School, Massachusetts; interview with Carol Darcy, principal, Atlantis Charter School, Massachusetts; interview with Thomas Commeret, head of school, Marblehead Community Charter Public School, Massachusetts; interview with Stephen Tracy, the Edison Project (the company managing Renaissance Charter School), Massachusetts.

8. Michigan Department of Education, "A Description of Michigan Public School Academies. 1995–96 Report to the House and Senate Committees in Education" (Lansing, 1996).

9. Mike Williams and Amber Arellano, "Universities Aren't Rushing to Get Charters; Cost, Work May Keep Many out of School Business," *Detroit Free Press*, January 24, 1994, sec. A. See also Joan Richardson, "Colleges Split on Charter Schools; Saginaw Valley State Goes Slow; CMU Zooms," *Detroit Free Press*, August 2, 1994, sec. B.

10. Ron Russell, "Central Michigan Plays a Key Role in Setting Up Programs," *Detroit News*, July 5, 1995.

11. Another possibility, of course, is that if CMU had not begun chartering schools across the state some other university might have stepped into the role of statewide chartering authority. So it is impossible to say with certainty that without CMU's aggressiveness nothing would have happened.

12. Interview with John Rhodes, Charter Schools Office, Georgia Department of Education.

13. Georgia Department of Education, "Georgia Charter School Program. Annual Report Summaries. School Year 1996–97" [sic: actually 1995–96], mimeograph, ca.1996; Georgia Department of Education, "State-Level Exemptions [received by charter schools]," mimeograph, ca.1996.

14. One theory, suggested by Robert Maranto based on his research on Arizona charter schools, is that charter high schools are less able to compete for "general" students because they cannot provide traditional high-school amenities like competitive athletics. Instead, they tend to focus on at-risk students and other niche populations. See Robert Maranto, Scott Milliman, Frederick Hess, and April Gresham, eds., *School Choice in the Real World: Lessons from Arizona Charter Schools* (Boulder, Colo.: Westview, 1999).

15. Massachusetts Executive Office of Education, Charter School Application 1996 (Boston, 1995); interview with Jim Peyser, undersecretary of education, Massachusetts.

16. Central Michigan University, *Charter School Application Materials* (Mt. Pleasant: CMU Charter Schools Office, 1995).

17. Mark Stevens, "Charter School Costs Viewed," *Denver Post,* February 11, 1994, sec. B; Kurt Hulse, "Clayton Charter School Application," memorandum to Wayne Eckerling, Denver Public Schools, December 17, 1993.

18. Interview with Meera Mani, head of school, Clayton Charter School, Colorado; interview with Adele Phelan, president, Clayton Foundation (parent organization of Clayton Charter School), Colorado.

19. Mark Stevens, "DPS Faces a Deficit of $15 Million; News May Spur Debate on Making Ends Meet," *Denver Post,* February 17, 1994, sec. B.

20. Denver Public Schools, "Minutes from Board of Education Meeting, February 17, 1994," mimeograph, 1994.

21. Interview with Rex Brown, principal, P.S. 1 Charter School, Colorado.

22. Mark Stevens, "State Board Directs New Look at P.S. 1," *Denver Post,* May 11, 1995, sec. B.

23. Mark Stevens, "Charters Win One, Lose One," *Denver Post,* June 9, 1995, sec. A.

24. Mark Stevens, "5 of 13 Charter Plans 'Merit Consideration.'" *Denver Post,* February 4, 1994, sec. B.

25. Denver Public Schools, "Minutes from Board of Education Meeting, February 17, 1994"; Stevens, "DPS Faces a Deficit of $15 Million."

26. Stevens, "Charter School Costs Viewed."

27. Thurgood Marshall Charter Middle School, "A Substitute Report on the Application for the Thurgood Marshall Charter Middle School, February 1, 1994," mimeograph, 1994; Denver Public Schools, "Reconsideration of Thurgood Marshall Charter Middle School Application," mimeograph, May 5, 1994.

28. Denver Public Schools, "Minutes from Board of Education Meeting, February 17, 1994."

29. Colorado State Board of Education, "Decision Reversing the Decision of the Denver County School District No. 1 and Remanding for Further Proceedings," mimeograph, April 6, 1994.

30. Denver Public Schools, "Minutes from Board of Education Meeting, May 19, 1994," mimeograph, 1994.

31. Colorado State Board of Education, "Final Decision Reversing the Decision of the Denver County School District No. 1 and Remanding for Further Proceedings," mimeograph, July 18, 1994.

32. George Lane, "State Ed Board's Role Lauded, Hit; Charter-School Actions Draw Mixed Reviews," *Denver Post,* March 1, 1995, sec. B; Stevens, "Charters Win One, Lose One," sec. A; Mark Stevens, "DPS Must Pursue Charter; Injunction Gives District Deadline for Negotiations with New School," *Denver Post,* March 28, 1995, sec. B.

33. The review team responding to the state's board's first 1994 remand wrote: "The review team continues to believe that the educational program of Thurgood Marshall has merit." Denver Public Schools, "District School Improvement and Accountability Council Report on Reconsideration of the Thurgood Marshall Charter School Application," mimeograph, May, 1994. The school board resolution rejecting the application a second time acknowledged "the community support of and interest in the educational philosophy" of the proposed school. Denver Public Schools, "Minutes from Board of Education Meeting, May 19, 1994," mimeograph, 1994. One consistent criticism of TMCMS's design was that it lacked uniqueness or innovativeness.

34. Allan Gottlieb, "DPS Lambasted by Lawmakers; Board Won't Open Charter School," *Denver Post,* October 17, 1995, sec. B.

35. It is important to point out that not all districts in Colorado have reacted in the same fashion to the charter school law. Some, notably Douglas County, have developed a reputation for working cooperatively with charter school applicants. Interview with Jim Griffin, executive director, Colorado League of Charter Schools; interview with Pat Grippe, assistant superintendent, Douglas County Public Schools, Colorado; Joy Fitzgerald, *Charter Schools in Colorado* (Denver: Colorado Children's Campaign, 1995), p. 12.

36. All of these schools, of course, were approved. So one reason they may have encountered little criticism of their educational approaches is that they proposed models that accorded with decisionmakers' preferences in the first place. It is conceivable that rejected applicants would report that the decisionmakers did object to aspects of their curriculum or pedagogy.

37. It will be interesting to see what concerns dominate school boards' debates over the *renewal* of charters, which has begun in Colorado, and over new charter proposals. It is possible that now charter schools are a reality in that state, questions about their educational value will become more prominent than they were in the initial approval process.

38. Colorado State Board of Education, *Revised Administrative Policy on Charter Schools* (August 11, 1994); Georgia Department of Education, "Charter Schools: Program Guidelines," mimeograph, 1995.

39. In Michigan, some charter schools are chartered by local boards. In these cases, of course, the schools *are* answerable to a local board. As noted in the previous section, though, only three of Michigan's 41 charter schools in 1995–96 were chartered locally; only two of Michigan's 521 local school districts had chartered schools.

40. Colorado Department of Education, "Waivers Granted to Charter Schools," mimeograph, January 17, 1996.

41. Interview with Peyser.

42. Interview with Robert Mills, director, Central Michigan University Charter Schools Office.

43. For an analysis of Colorado's education law, see Bryan Hassel, "Designed to Fail? Charter Schools and the Politics of Structural Choice," Ph.D. dissertation, Harvard University, 1997.

44. This section draws on Massachusetts Executive Office of Education, "Public School Statutes and Regulations. Charter Schools Memo 95-13," memorandum to charter schools, August 17, 1995, which details the public school statutes and regulations that apply to charter schools, on other legal and technical advisories issued by the Massachusetts Executive Office of Education on specific aspects of law, and on a review of the Massachusetts General Laws.

45. Massachusetts General Laws, chap. 71, sec. 1.

46. Ibid., secs. 2, 13D, 13F, 48, 50.

47. Since the period covered by this study, Massachusetts has developed statewide standards, curriculum frameworks, and assessments in the core subjects of mathematics, science and technology, history and social science, English, foreign languages, and the arts. The standards "set forth the skills, competencies, and knowledge expected to be possessed by all students." The curriculum frameworks "present broad pedagogical approaches and strategies to assisting students in developing the skills, competencies and

knowledge called for by these standards" (Massachusetts General Laws, chap. 69). Charter schools are subject to these standards and frameworks.

48. Massachusetts General Laws, chap. 70, sec. 8.

49. Ibid., chap. 30b, chap. 149.

50. It is interesting that many (though not all) of these restrictions did not result from state legislative compromises but were imposed by federal law and regulation.

51. Interview with Ed Davis, principal, Charles Ellis Montessori Academy, Georgia.

52. At the end of the 1995–96 school year, only Arizona and California had more charter schools than any of these states. Minnesota was slightly ahead of Massachusetts, with 16 schools open. But Minnesota's charter law passed in 1991, and schools there proliferated more slowly than in Massachusetts. California's law is also older (1992), and California is so large that the number of charter schools there was proportionally smaller than in these three states.

53. Karl E. Weick, "Educational Organizations as Loosely Coupled Systems," *Administrative Sciences Quarterly,* vol. 21 (1976), pp. 1–19; John M. Meyer and Brian Rowan, "Institutionalized Organizations: Formal Structure as Myth and Ceremony," *American Journal of Sociology,* vol. 83 (September 1977), pp. 340–63.

Chapter Five

1. In addition to missing out on economies of scale, there are other fiscal disadvantages of independence. One is that charter schools look significantly riskier to lenders, property owners, and other types of investors than traditional school districts do. All else equal, independent charter schools will pay a "risk premium" when they borrow money or sign leases.

2. PPOR comprises revenues from state and local property taxes for operations and thus excludes certain important categories of school district revenue, including federal funds, interest on reserves, and funding for school construction and renovation. In 1993–94, for example, average PPOR was $4,214, but total per-pupil spending averaged $6,476. So PPOR was just 65 percent of total per-pupil spending; 80 percent of PPOR was just 52 percent of total per-pupil spending. See Byron Pendley, "State Average per-Pupil Spending," memorandum to Bill Windler, Denver, August 22, 1995.

3. Private-school conversions had even lower per-pupil expenses, with a mean of just $5,299.

4. RPP International, *A National Study of Charter Schools: Second Year Report* (Washington: U.S. Office of Educational Research and Improvement, 1998), p. 94.

5. This finding also echoes the national charter school study. Private school conversions responding to that study listed "financial reasons" and "to attract students" as their most important reasons for founding a charter school, while newly created schools listed "to serve special population" and "to realize an alternative vision." Ibid., p. 78.

6. Jordana Hart, "Money, Space Hinder Mass. Charter Schools," *Boston Globe,* October 25, 1994; Jordana Hart, "Charter Schools Get Nod to Open; 14 Get State Backing; Edison Project Short," *Boston Globe,* December 10, 1994; Debra Sue Wong, "3 of 17 Charter Schools Won't Open This Year; Neighborhood House, Pacific Rim Shoot for '96," *Boston Globe,* May 31, 1995.

7. Alexander Reid, "Charter School Off to an Unconventional Start; Innovative Program Is Held in Hull Motel," *Boston Globe*, September 17, 1995, South Weekly Section.

8. Tom Loveless and Claudia Jasin, "Starting from Scratch: Political and Organizational Challenges Facing Charter Schools," *Educational Administration Quarterly*, vol. 34 (February 1998), pp. 9–30.

9. Ron Russell, "Central Michigan Plays a Key Role in Setting Up Programs," *Detroit News*, July 5, 1995.

10. Wong, "3 of 17 Charter Schools Won't Open This Year."

11. Hart, "Money, Space Hinder Mass. Charter Schools"; Hart, "Charter Schools Get Nod to Open."

12. The national charter school study also found that facilities issues loomed large for charter schools, especially those that were newly created. RPP International, *A National Study of Charter Schools*, p. 94.

13. Allan Odden, *Rethinking School Finance* (San Francisco: Jossey-Bass, 1992).

14. Massachusetts Executive Office of Education, "Special Education. Charter Schools Memo 95-3," memorandum to charter schools, April 27, 1995.

15. Massachusetts Department of Education, *The Massachusetts Charter School Initiative. 1996 Report* (Boston, 1996).

16. Pendley, "State Average per-Pupil Spending."

17. Interview with Pat Grippe, assistant superintendent, Douglas County Schools, Colorado. Douglas County Schools, "Learning Services. Charter School Funding 1995–96 (per Pupil Cost)," mimeograph, 1995.

18. Massachusetts Department of Education, "The Massachusetts Charter School Initiative. 1996 Report."

19. P.S. 1, *Getting Started. 1995–96 Annual Report* (Denver: Urban Learning Communities, 1996).

20. Interviews with all schools.

21. Michigan State Board of Education, "Partnership Agreement [between the State Board of Education and the Michigan Partnership for New Education]," mimeograph, 1995.

22. Central Michigan University Resource Center for Charter Schools, *Annual Report Period Ending June 30, 1996* (Mt. Pleasant, 1996).

23. Interview with Jim Griffin, executive director, Colorado League of Charter Schools.

24. Colorado Department of Education, *Charter Schools Information Packet*, 3d ed. (Denver, January 1995).

25. Interview with Linda Brown, director, Charter School Resource Center, Pioneer Institute; Pioneer Institute for Public Policy Research, *Massachusetts Charter School Handbook*, 2d ed. (Boston, 1996).

Chapter Six

1. Ted Kolderie, *The Charter Idea: Update and Prospects, Fall '95*, Public Services Redesign Project (St. Paul, Minn.: Center for Policy Studies, 1995).

2. As laboratories, charter schools would play a similar role to structures within existing school districts, such as experimental schools, some magnet schools, and the like.

3. The national charter school study reports that approximately one in five charter schools in 1996–97 served a population in which almost all students were children of color, economically disadvantaged, or students with disabilities. RPP International, *A National Study of Charter Schools: Second Year Report* (Washington: U.S. Department of Education, 1998).

4. Eric Rofes, *How Are School Districts Responding to Charter Laws and Charter Schools?* (Policy Analysis for California Education, University of California at Berkeley, 1998).

5. Robert Maranto, Scott Milliman, Frederick Hess, and April Gresham, "Arizona Charter Schools and District Schools," in Robert Maranto, Scott Milliman, Frederick Hess, and April Gresham, eds., *School Choice in the Real World: Lessons from Arizona Charter Schools* (Boulder, Colo.: Westview, 1999).

6. It is important to make a distinction between "innovative" and "distinctive." Charter schools are often quite different from neighboring public schools. But they may not be innovative if they resemble other schools elsewhere. Thus to say that a school is not innovative is not to say that it is providing a service that would be otherwise available locally. As one report on charter schools noted, "If you crave tea and all the local restaurant serves is coffee, the opening of a cafe stocked with Darjeeling and Oolong can look like an extraordinary breakthrough" (Chester E. Finn Jr., Bruno V. Manno, and Louann Bierlein, *Charter Schools in Action: What Have We Learned?* (Washington: Hudson Institute, 1996).

7. One reason why charter schools' curriculums and practices do not look radically different from prevailing norms is perhaps their ultimate accountability to parents. Though charter-choosing parents may be looking for options different from those offered by conventional public schools, most are not eager for their children to become the subjects of experiments.

8. Rosenblum Brigham Associates, *Innovation and Massachusetts Charter Schools* (Boston: Massachusetts Department of Education, 1998). The study did find a handful of specific practices that were much more common in charter schools than in district schools, including extended-day programs, performance-based compensation for staffs, parent contracts, and individual learning plans for all students.

9. Some of the responses to charter schools Rofes detected were actually changes in *state* policies regarding school-based management and school finance, as well as changes in district practices regarding "reconstitution" of failing schools and school accountability systems. Rofes, *How Are School Districts Responding?* pp. 21–22.

10. Richard F. Elmore, "Getting to Scale with Good Educational Practice," *Harvard Educational Review,* vol. 66 (Spring 1996), pp. 1–26.

11. New American Schools, *Getting Stronger and Stronger: New American Schools Annual Report* (Arlington, Va., 1996); Susan J. Bodily and others, *Designing New American Schools: Baseline Observations on Nine Design Teams* (Santa Monica, Calif.: Rand, 1995).

12. Susan J. Bodily and others, *Lessons from the New American Schools' Scale-Up Phase: Prospects for Bringing Designs to Multiple Schools* (Santa Monica, Calif.: Rand, 1998).

13. Rofes's study of 25 school districts and their responses to charter schools casts additional doubt on the laboratory thesis: "Few superintendents, principals and teachers in district schools were thinking of charter schools as educational laboratories or attempting to transfer pedagogical innovations from charters to the district schools." Rofes, *How Are School Districts Responding?* p. 13.

14. National Center for Education Statistics, *Digest of Educational Statistics* (Washington: U.S. Government Printing Office, 1995), table 95.

15. Robert Antonucci, "Charter School Reimbursement," memorandum to State Board of Education, Massachusetts Commissioner of Education, January 3, 1997.

16. Joan Richardson, "Lawsuit Targets Charter School; Academy Would Run Home School Network," *Detroit Free Press,* August 18, 1994, sec. B; Joan Richardson, "Judge Halts Charter School Funding; Foes Say Support for Nonpublic Schools May Defy Constitution," *Detroit Free Press,* October 20, 1994, sec. B; Joan Richardson, "Judge Strikes Down Charter-School Law; Engler, Supporters Promise to Fight," *Detroit Free Press,* November 2, 1994, sec. A; Joan Richardson, "Charter School Funds Approved; Lawmakers Also Revise Law to Try to Address Judge's Concerns," *Detroit Free Press,* December 15, 1994, sec. B. In Massachusetts and Colorado, parents filed lawsuits challenging the charter law or specific actions taken pursuant to it. These lawsuits were not successful, and they were not filed by districts. In fact, a school district was the *defendant* in the Pueblo, Colorado, case after closing two existing public schools and simultaneously opening a charter school. On the Massachusetts case, see Laura Goodman et al., "Complaint," filed in Commonwealth of Massachusetts, Essex, Superior Court Department of the Trial Court, Civil Action No. 95-1440b, 1995; Jordana Hart, "Lawsuit Challenges Charter Schools," *Boston Globe,* June 23, 1995; Paul Langner, "Charter School Foes Lose Court Ruling," *Boston Globe,* July 1, 1995.

17. Richard McClellan, "A Preliminary Outline of the Charter School Changes in Senate Bill 679," mimeograph prepared for Central Michigan University, 1995.

18. The U.S. Department of Education's charter study found that local political challenges were among the principal difficulties faced by many charter schools. RPP International and the University of Minnesota, *A Study of Charter Schools* (Washington: U.S. Department of Education, 1997).

19. Tom Loveless and Claudia Jasin, "Starting from Scratch: Political and Organizational Challenges Facing Charter Schools," *Educational Administration Quarterly,* vol. 34 (February 1998), p. 24.

20. Alleged harassment was reported by Loveless and Jasin, "Starting from Scratch," p. 21.

21. Interview with John Correiro, board member, Atlantis Charter School, Massachusetts.

22. Brendan Farrington, "Temple Defends Decision on Lease," *Patriot Ledger,* May 13, 1996, sec. S.

23. Joan Richardson, "Union Pressures State University over Charter Schools," *Detroit Free Press,* June 6, 1994, sec. A.

24. Joan Richardson, "District Won't Sell Building for Charter School," *Detroit Free Press,* September 27, 1994, sec. B. In both states, charter schools alleged other actions on the part of school districts that they could not document. For example, one charter school accused local district officials of pressuring building inspectors not to approve charter school facilities for occupancy.

25. Loveless and Jasin, "Starting from Scratch," p. 20.

26. Janet Bingham, "Charter School Money a Trade-Off; Public Education Could Suffer When Funds Spent on Alternatives," *Denver Post,* February 15, 1994, sec. B.

27. Mark Stevens, "Programs May Be Cut by DPS; Grim Budget Picture Shown to School Board," *Denver Post,* May 19, 1995, sec. B. In the federal government, this perverse practice of cutting successful programs first has become known as the "Washing-

ton Monument strategy," after the Department of Interior's "offer" to trim its budget by closing the Washington Monument, which provoked angry calls and letters to members of Congress from would-be tourists.

28. Albert O. Hirschman, *Exit, Voice, and Loyalty: Responses to Decline in Firms, Organizations, and States* (Harvard University Press, 1970), pp. 59–60. Emphasis in original.

29. Rofes finds evidence of similar thinking on the part of school districts: "One unexpected finding of this research was that both school district employees and charter school leaders were aware that charters often attract families with a long history of complaints against the local school district and students who have had disciplinary problems in the traditional public schools." Rofes, *How Are School Districts Responding?* p. 6.

30. Interview with Pat Grippe, assistant superintendent, Douglas County Public Schools, Colorado.

31. Rofes, *How Are School Districts Responding?* pp. 2, 18–21.

32. Maranto et al., "Arizona Charter Schools and District Schools."

33. See, for example, Joe Nathan, *Charter Schools: Creating Hope and Opportunity for American Education* (San Francisco: Jossey-Bass, 1996), pp. 85–87.

34. William Windler, "Colorado's Charter Schools: A Spark for Change and a Catalyst for Reform," mimeograph, ca. 1995, pp. 3–4.

35. Mary Anne Raywid, "The Struggles and Joys of Trailblazing," *Phi Delta Kappan*, vol. 76 (March 1995), pp. 555–60; Nathan, *Charter Schools*, pp. 87–88. Most of these anecdotes describe circumstances in which districts emulated the institutional arrangements under which charter schools work rather than specific curricula or instructional approaches. This experience supports the previous section's argument that the institutional arrangements in which charters function are the program's most significant innovation, the one most likely to diffuse.

36. Nathan, *Charter Schools*, pp. 88–92; Pioneer Institute for Public Policy Research, "Charter Schools: Fears and Facts," *Policy Directions*, no. 1 (April 1995).

37. See, for example, James Champy, *Reengineering Management: The Mandate for New Leadership* (New York: HarperBusiness, 1995).

Chapter Seven

1. These 35 laws included 34 states and the District of Columbia. For simplicity, hereafter I refer to these 35 jurisdictions as "35 states."

2. Amendments to California's law in 1998 made it clear that charter schools could incorporate as independent nonprofits.

3. In 1998, Georgia opened up the process to schools that were not conversions of existing public schools. And in 1997, Massachusetts raised (but did not eliminate) its cap on the number of charter schools.

4. For a detailed examination of charter schools' support needs, see Marc Dean Millot, *A Nonprofit Technical Assistance Activity for Charter Applicants in Pennsylvania: Mission, Functions, Capability, and Plans* (Seattle, Wash.: Rand Institute for Education and Training, 1996).

5. Bruno V. Manno and others, *Charter School Accountability: Problems and Prospects*, part IV of Chester E. Finn Jr. and others, *Charter Schools in Action: A Final Report* (Washington: Hudson Institute, 1997), p. 1.

Index